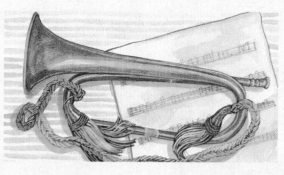

HYMNS OF PRAISE

HYMNS OF PRAISE

Pamela J. Kennedy

IDEALS PUBLICATIONS, A DIVISION OF GUIDEPOSTS
NASHVILLE, TENNESSEE

ISBN 0-8249-4126-8

Copyright © 2001 by Ideals Publications, a Division of Guideposts
Text copyright © 2001 by Pamela Kennedy

Published by Ideals Publications, a Division of Guideposts
535 Metroplex Drive, Suite 250
Nashville, TN 37211
www.idealspublications.com

Library of Congress Cataloging-in-Publication Data
Kennedy, Pamela, 1946–
    Hymns of praise / Pamela Kennedy.
        p. cm.
    Includes index.
    ISBN 0-8249-4126-8 (alk. paper)
    1. Hymns, English—History and criticism. 2.Hymns, English—
United States—History and criticism. I. Title.

BV315 .K37 2001
264'23'09—dc21   2001016580

10 8 6 4 2 1 3 5 7 9

PUBLISHER, PATRICIA A. PINGRY
BOOK DESIGNER, EVE DEGRIE
COPY EDITOR, ELIZABETH KEA
COPY EDITOR AND PERMISSIONS, AMY JOHNSON

PHOTOGRAPHY BY CARR CLIFTON

Cover Photo by Superstock

ACKNOWLEDGMENTS:

ALEXANDER, CECIL F. and SANDERSON, L.O. "All Things Bright and Beautiful."
Copyright © 1935. Renewal 1963 by Gospel Advocate Company, Leon Sanderson,
Owner. All Rights Reserved. Reprinted by permission. CHISHOLM, THOMAS O. and
RUNYAN, WILLIAM M. "Great Is Thy Faithfulness." Copyright © 1923. Renewal 1951
Hope Publishing Co., Carol Stream, IL 60188. All rights reserved. Used by permis-
sion. MIEIR, AUDREY. "His Name Is Wonderful." Copyright © 1959. Renewed 1987
by Manna Music, Inc., 35255 Brooten Road, Pacific City, OR 97135. All Rights
Reserved. Used by Permission.

All possible care has been taken to fully acknowledge the ownership and use of every
selection in this book. If any mistakes or omissions have occurred, they will be cor-
rected in subsequent editions, provided notification is sent to the publisher.

For the Lord, who is the Singer
and for Kraig, who taught me the song.
P.J.K.

Stand Up, Stand Up for Jesus
George Duffield Jr., 1818—1888

NOT AFRAID TO STAND ALONE

In 1858, the city of Philadelphia was swept with a city-wide religious awakening, and the media dubbed the phenomenon "the Work of God in Philadelphia." Ministers of all denominations were seeing their congregations swell with both newly converted and re-dedicated Christian believers. One of the most powerful of the Philadelphia preachers was Dudley Tyng, a twenty-nine-year-old Episcopalian. Tyng was the son of a successful preacher, the Reverend Stephen H. Tyng, and had a natural entrée into his father's pulpit at the Church of the Epiphany. Because he served as his father's assistant, it seemed only natural that the young man, upon his pastor-father's retirement, would succeed him as the congregation's spiritual leader. The congregation, however, was not as enthusiastic about their pastor's replacement.

Unlike his father, the younger Tyng eschewed tact in favor of direct and forceful doctrinal preaching. Not only did his style ruffle some congregational feathers, but his outspoken and uncompromising stand against slavery offended many of the long-time members. Before long, there was a grassroots movement to remove the young pastor. Dudley was not without a following, however, and when he resigned his post as rector at the Church of the Epiphany, a small group of friends went with him. Together they established a new congregation they called the Church of the Covenant with Tyng as their minister.

Despite their small beginnings and lack of a formal church building, the small group grew quickly. In addition to his Sunday meetings, Pastor Tyng began holding meetings for men at the local YMCA during weekday lunch hours. Within months, thousands were attending these meetings to hear the dynamic young preacher.

Tyng's goal was always that his listeners live out their faith daily. On one Tuesday afternoon in March of 1858, Dudley preached a sermon from the text of Exodus 10:11, ending with the rousing cry, "Go now ye that are men and serve the Lord." At the close of the service more than one thousand men indicated their desire to commit their lives to serve Christ. In an attempt to encourage them with his own devotion to the Lord, the pastor declared that he would rather lose his right arm than fall short of his duty in preaching God's Word. Little did he realize how prophetic those words would be.

Only a week later, Dudley Tyng was visiting a farm in the nearby countryside. As he observed a corn thrasher operating in a barn, the sleeve of his shirt became caught between the cogs and his right arm was pulled into the machinery and nearly severed. Despite the efforts of physicians to repair the damaged arm, it became infected. Loss of blood, septic infection, and shock combined to take the life of the young preacher on April 19, 1858, just twenty days after his most successful sermon.

Just before his death, Dudley was visited by a group of sorrowful friends and fellow pastors. Observing their grief, he urged them to sing a hymn of faith, then weakly began the first verse of "Rock of Ages." Tearfully, his father leaned over and asked if his dying son had any last words to share with his loved ones. Looking upon the group with his last bit of strength, the young man whispered: "Tell them to stand up for Jesus!"

In attendance at that touching bedside scene was one of Dudley's dearest friends and colleagues, Reverend George Duffield. Struck by the simplicity and conviction of his friend's last words, Duffield decided to make them the centerpiece of his sermon the following week. He chose for his text Ephesians 6:14: "Stand therefore, having your loins girt about with truth, and having on the breastplate of righteousness." Reverend Duffield concluded his message with a poem he had written. It was the six-stanza verse we know as "Stand Up, Stand Up for Jesus." Duffield's Sunday school superintendent was so impressed with the poem that he had it printed and distributed to all his students. Within a short time, it was circulated in a Baptist periodical and eventually set to music. Since that time it has served to inspire and encourage Christians of all denominations to take a stand for Jesus. Today we may not recall the words Dudley Tyng preached from his pulpit; but whenever this inspiring hymn is sung, the message he whispered from his deathbed echoes once more.

Stand Up, Stand Up for Jesus

George Duffield Jr.

George J. Webb

1. Stand up, stand up for Je - sus, Ye sol - diers of the cross; Lift
2. Stand up, stand up for Je - sus, Stand in His strength a - lone; The
3. Stand up, stand up for Je - sus, The strife will not be long; This

high His roy - al ban - ner, It must not suf - fer loss: From
arm of flesh will fail you, Ye dare not trust your own: Put
day the noise of bat - tle, The next the vic - tor's song: To

vic - t'ry un - to vic - t'ry His ar - my shall He lead, Till
on the gos - pel ar - mor, Each piece put on with prayer; Where
him that o - ver - com - eth A crown of life shall be; He,

ev - 'ry foe is van - quished, And Christ is Lord in - deed.
du - ty calls or dan - ger, Be nev - er want - ing there.
with the King of glo - ry, Shall reign e - ter - nal - ly.

Come, Thou Fount of Every Blessing
Robert Robinson, 1735–1790

SONG FROM A WANDERING HEART

Life was bleak in Swaffham, Norfolk, England—especially for the fatherless and poor. Such was the case for young Robert Robinson. After the death of his father, eight-year-old Robert had little direction. He avoided school as much as possible and, instead, spent time getting into trouble with his friends. Concerned about her young son's future, Robert's mother sent her teenage son to apprentice as a barber in London.

His tutor and guardian, Joseph Anderson, had little success interesting young Robert in the barbering trade. London had many more opportunities for mischief than small Swaffham, and the young apprentice soon joined up with a notorious gang of troublemakers. Despite Anderson's stern reprimands and severe punishments, Robert spent most of his hours on the streets, involved in every kind of unsavory activity. He drank to excess and stole from shopkeepers. Joseph Anderson was only too glad when the five years of apprenticeship came to an end and he could be rid of his troublesome charge.

Freed from the constraints of his training, Robinson had even more time for his friends and their adventures. Apparently bored with their regular pursuits, the band of young men decided to attend one of the many open-air evangelistic meetings being held in London during the winter of 1754. Their intent, however, was not to receive spiritual enlightenment but to heckle the preacher. Little did Robert Robinson suspect that he would leave the meeting a changed young man.

The speaker giving the message that cold December day was George Whitefield, a dynamic Methodist preacher with a message that warned his listeners of the "wrath to come" for those who chose to ignore the call of God upon their lives. Something in the preacher's words struck a chord in the rebellious Robinson, and by the end of the service, he had decided to accept the preacher's call to believe in Christ.

Within a few years, Robert Robinson had not only turned his life over to God; he also decided to become a Methodist minister and follow in the footsteps of his inspiration, George Whitefield. Although he began his preaching career in the Methodist church, he subsequently moved to Cambridge. There he found that his theology was more in keeping with the Baptist traditions, and he became a Baptist pastor.

Although schoolwork had only been a burden and a bore for him as a child, Robert had a keen mind; as a preacher and teacher, he wrote inspiring sermons, theological papers, religious poetry, and hymns. It was the practice for ministers of his day to conclude their sermons with hymn-poems. When he was only twenty-three, Robert penned the words of the hymn we know as "Come, Thou Fount of Every Blessing." In the verses praising God's never-ceasing mercy and grace, the author recounts how his heart is prone to wander away from God. Perhaps the "old Robert" was never far from the preacher's memory.

It is said that when he was a young man, just beginning his ministry as a pastor, Robert prayed that when he died he would go "softly, suddenly, and silently" to be with his Maker. When he was only fifty-four, God answered that prayer. Robinson had been called to Birmingham to fill the pulpit for a well-known preacher, Dr. Priestly. The morning after arriving at Priestly's home, he failed to join the minister for breakfast. Concerned, Dr. Priestly rapped at his guest's door. When there was no answer, the host entered the room to find that Robinson had died in bed, apparently just as he had desired—softly and silently. While he may have slipped away quietly, the words of Robert Robinson still echo in our churches centuries later. In them we still find comfort in the reassurance that whenever we are tempted to wander, God's grace is able to hold us fast.

With my whole heart have I sought thee:
O let me not wander from thy commandments.
Thy word have I hid in mine heart,
that I might not sin against thee. Psalm 119:10–11

Come, Thou Fount of Every Blessing

Robert Robinson

John Wyeth

1. Come, Thou Fount of ev-'ry bless-ing, Tune my heart to sing Thy grace;
2. Here I raise my Eb-e-ne-zer, Hith-er by Thy help I'm come;
3. O to grace how great a debt-or Dai-ly I'm con-strained to be!

Streams of mer-cy, nev-er ceas-ing, Call for songs of loud-est praise.
And I hope, by Thy good plea-sure, Safe-ly to ar-rive at home.
Let Thy good-ness, like a fet-ter, Bind my wan-d'ring heart to Thee.

Teach me some me-lo-dious son-net, Sung by flam-ing tongues a-bove.
Je-sus sought me when a stran-ger, Wan-d'ring from the fold of God;
Prone to wan-der, Lord I feel it, Prone to leave the God I love;

Praise the mount–I'm fixed up-on it– Mount of Thy re-deem-ing love.
He, to res-cue me from dan-ger, In-ter-posed His pre-cious blood.
Here's my heart, O take and seal it, Seal it for Thy courts a-bove.

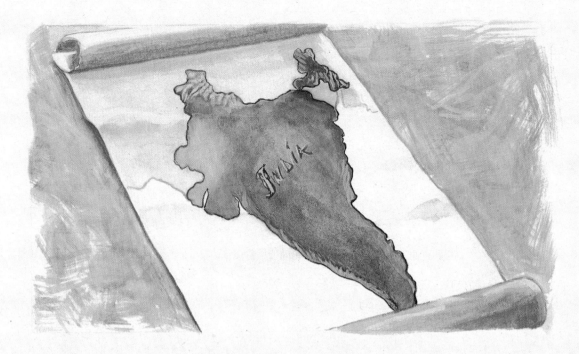

O Worship the King
Robert Grant, 1779–1838

A GOVERNOR WORSHIPS HIS KING

Today we often discover that our governmental leaders are reluctant to mix their religion and their politics. In eighteenth- and nineteenth-century India, this was not the case. Charles Grant, a respected ranking leader in the Indian government and a director of the East India Company, was an outspoken member of the evangelical wing of the Anglican Church. In Bengal, where he made his home, he was well-known as a man of faith and integrity. When his son Robert was born in 1779, Charles took care to bring him up in "the nurture and admonition of the Lord."

It appeared that Robert Grant was well suited to follow in his father's footsteps. He demonstrated a keen mind, a devout spirit, and a heart for both God and his fellow man. He also showed aptitude in business and politics and, at the age of fifty-five, was appointed governor of Bombay, India.

In addition to his passion for politics, Grant demonstrated a fervor for missions and invested his resources to support the missionary outreach of the church. His contributions did much to enrich the lives of the citizens of Bombay in a variety of ways; and after his death, the people of India established a medical college in his name as a lasting memorial.

Despite his good works and religious devotion, few people living outside India have ever heard of Robert Grant. Christians all over the world, however, have sung his words of tribute to God. Written in 1833 and published by his brother Charles a year after Robert's death, the poem "O Worship the King" stands as a testimony to the One whom Robert honored more than all of his earthly accolades. The poetry of this hymn contains some of the richest imagery ever written describing God's majesty and power. Consider the vivid word pictures illustrating the power of God in the following verse:

> O tell of His might, O sing of His grace,
> Whose robe is the light, whose canopy space;
> His chariots of wrath the deep thunderclouds form,
> And dark is His path on the wings of the storm.

Grant's use of seven different titles for God—King, Shield, Defender, Ancient of Days, Maker, Redeemer, Friend—plumbs the depths of the character of his Creator. "O Worship the King" has often been used as the model for worship hymns because its verses blend in poetic harmony both the majestic and intimate nature of God.

With such an inspiring and eloquent text, the challenge for those setting sacred poems to music is to discover or create a melody that matches the words in both mood and tone. The tune selected for Grant's poem was one adapted from a composition by the son of an Austrian carriage wheel maker, and it was written years before Grant's text. The composer was well-known for his symphonies and religious music and was famous as one of the talented Haydn brothers of Vienna.

Many of Robert Grant's sacred poems have been forgotten, but this magnificent work, matched by the triumphant melody of Johann Michael Haydn, lives on as one of the most famous hymns in Christendom.

Lift up your heads, O ye gates;
even lift them up, ye everlasting doors;
and the King of glory shall come in.
Who is this King of glory? The Lord of hosts,
he is the King of glory. Psalm 24:9–10

O Worship the King

Robert Grant

Johann M. Haydn

1. O wor - ship the King, all - glo - rious a - bove,
2. O tell of His might, O sing of His grace,
3. Thy boun - ti - ful care what tongue can re - cite?
4. Frail chil - dren of dust, and fee - ble as frail,

O grate - ful - ly sing His pow - er and His love;
Whose robe is the light, whose can - o - py space.
It breathes in the air, it shines in the light,
In Thee do we trust, nor find Thee to fail;

Our Shield and De - fend - er, the An - cient of Days,
His char - iots of wrath the deep thun - der - clouds form,
It streams from the hills, it de - scends to the plain,
Thy mer - cies how ten - der! how firm to the end!

Pa - vil - ioned in splen - dor, and gird - ed with praise.
And dark is His path on the wings of the storm.
And sweet - ly dis - tills in the dew and the rain.
Our Mak - er, De - fend - er, Re - deem - er, and Friend.

There Is a Fountain
William Cowper, 1731—1800

STRENGTH DESPITE WEAKNESS

William Cowper was born in Great Berkhamstead, England, on November 15, 1731. From his earliest days, William was small and physically frail; and after his mother's death when he was only six years old, his emotional state became extremely fragile as well. He was bright, however, and pursued academics with great success.

His father, an English clergyman, encouraged William to study law. It seemed a good match for the studious young man, and he completed his classes with high grades. Upon completion of his degree, however, there remained one hurdle: the final examination before the bar. Plagued by a fear of speaking in public, William could only stammer before succumbing to a complete mental breakdown. He never completed his bar examination and, thus, never practiced his profession. In fact, the desperate young man went on to attempt suicide and was eventually committed to an insane asylum, where he languished for over eighteen months.

During the dreary months Cowper spent in the institution for the mentally disturbed, he turned to the Scriptures for solace. One day, he read the text of Romans 3:24–25. It was as if the words were written specifically for him and his whole life was changed in an instant.

Being justified freely by his grace through the redemption that is in Christ Jesus: Whom God hath set forth to be a propitiation through faith in his blood, to declare his righteousness for the remission of sins that are past, through the forbearance of God.

William accepted the words as a promise from God and turned his life over to the lordship of Jesus Christ.

After his religious conversion, Cowper's mental state began to improve and he was released from the institution. His melancholia never completely left; but with the care and friendship of the Reverend and Mrs. Morley Unwin, William found the family and security his early life lacked. A frequent visitor to the Unwin's was the converted slave trader, John Newton, who wrote the beloved hymn "Amazing Grace." He and Cowper became friends. When Unwin passed away, Newton persuaded Cowper, Unwin's recent widow, and her entire family to move to Olney, England, where Newton pastored the local Anglican Church. Their proximity and common interests allowed Newton and Cowper to develop a close friendship.

Encouraged by his newfound mentor, Cowper began to write in earnest. The words that had been so difficult to speak found a release as he set pen to paper; and despite recurring bouts of depression, he managed to produce a translation of Homer and volumes of poems, some of which literary critics have rated technically comparable to Pope and Shelley. In addition to his secular works, Cowper collaborated with Newton in the writing of hymns for Newton's weekly prayer meetings. Eventually their work was collected and published as the famous *Olney Hymns*.

It was during this time that William Cowper recalled the text from Romans that had precipitated his conversion. Combining these verses with an Old Testament text from Zechariah 13:1 that refers to a "fountain opened to the house of David and to the inhabitants of Jerusalem for sin and uncleanliness," Cowper penned the moving verses of his hymn "There Is a Fountain." In its last verse is a poignant reminder of the author's own struggles: "When this poor lisping, stamm'ring tongue lies silent in the grave / Then in a nobler, sweeter song, I'll sing Thy pow'r to save."

His hymn confidently speaks of God's power to redeem and restore the most guilty of sinners; and over the past two centuries, many have been strengthened by its powerful message. Ironically, it is said that Cowper himself lacked the assurance of God's grace. Whether it resulted from his recurring bouts of depression or from some inner spiritual struggle, he frequently despaired over the weakness of his own faith. It appears, however, that his lifelong struggle with doubt came to an end a mere half-hour before he died. Those present at his deathbed reported that William's face lit up with a smile minutes before he passed away; and in an attitude of wonder he whispered, "I am not shut out of heaven after all." Perhaps he had at last glimpsed that heavenly fountain.

There Is a Fountain

William Cowper

Traditional

1. There is a foun-tain filled with blood Drawn from Im-man - uel's veins;
2. The dy - ing thief re-joiced to see That foun-tain in his day;
3. Dear dy - ing Lamb, Thy pre - cious blood Shall nev - er lose its power,
4. E'er since by faith I saw the stream Thy flow-ing wounds sup - ply,

And sin - ners, plunged be - neath that flood Lose all their guilt - y stains:
And there may I, though vile as he, Wash all my sins a-way:
Till all the ran-somed church of God Be saved to sin no more:
Re - deem - ing love has been my theme, And shall be till I die:

Lose all their guilt - y stains, Lose all their guilt - y stains;
Wash all my sins a - way, Wash all my sins a - way;
Be saved, to sin no more, Be saved, to sin no more;
And shall be till I die, And shall be till I die;

And sin-ners, plunged be - neath that flood, Lose all their guilt-y stains.
And there may I, though vile as he, Wash all my sins a - way.
Till all the ran-somed church of God Be saved, to sin no more.
Re - deem - ing love has been my theme, And shall be till I die.

'Tis So Sweet to Trust in Jesus

Louisa M. Stead, 1850–1917

FROM TRAGEDY TO TRUST

For as long as she could remember, young Louisa felt the call to be a missionary. Upon completion of her education at the age of twenty-one, she left her home in Dover, England, and traveled to the United States where she settled for a time in Cincinnati, Ohio. After serving the Lord for four years in Ohio, Louisa met and married a Mr. Stead in 1875. The couple rejoiced at the birth of their first child, a daughter they named Lily, and the young family basked in the joy of its blessings.

When Lily was four years old, her parents traveled to Long Island, New York. One day they packed a picnic lunch and took it to the beach. As they sat talking, laughing, and enjoying their meal together, they heard the unmistakable cries of someone in distress. Jumping up, Mr. Stead spotted a boy several yards out to sea, struggling to stay above water. Without thought of his own safety, the young father plunged into the water and swam to the drowning boy. Panic-stricken, the boy grasped frantically at his rescuer; and as Louisa and Lily looked on helplessly, both the boy and the man plunged below the waves and drowned.

Grief-stricken, the young widow and her daughter struggled through the days immediately following the death of their husband and father. Crying out to the God she had always trusted, Louisa's anguished "Why?" seemed to be answered by a quiet assurance, and she wrote these words in her journal:

> 'Tis so sweet to trust in Jesus, just to take Him at His word:
> Just to rest upon His promise; just to know, 'Thus saith the Lord.'
> Jesus, Jesus, How I trust Him! How I've proved Him o'er and o'er!
> Jesus, Jesus, precious Jesus! O for grace to trust Him more!

Penned originally as a poem expressing her personal passage from questioning to confidence, the words weren't given a wider audience until 1882. Influential nineteenth-century composer and publisher William James Kirkpatrick wrote an original melody specifically for Louisa Stead's text, and the new hymn was included in a collection entitled *Songs of Triumph* compiled by Kirkpatrick and his colleague, John R. Sweeney.

Alone now with her young daughter, Louisa's fervor to be a missionary rekindled. Packing her belongings, she moved to South Africa and threw herself into the mission work there. Before long, God brought a Methodist minister into her life, and Louisa married the South African native Robert Wodehouse. Together they served on the mission field until Louisa's failing health made it necessary for the family to return to America in 1895. While Louisa recuperated, Robert served as the pastor of a Methodist church. After five years, Louisa had regained enough strength for the couple to return to their beloved Africa. This time, however, they settled at a mission station in Umtali, Southern Rhodesia. Lily, now in her early twenties, joined her family in Africa and with her husband, D.A. Carson, served alongside her mother. When ill health once again forced Louisa to curtail her missionary work, she decided to stay on in Africa. She moved to the family home in Penkridge, about fifty miles from the missionary station in Umtali, where she remained until her death at the age of sixty-seven on January 18, 1917.

Louisa's life had not been easy; but despite her grief, physical suffering, and exhaustion, her indomitable spirit encouraged those around her. In a letter composed at Umtali she once wrote:

> In connection with this whole mission there are glorious possibilities, but one cannot, in the face of the peculiar difficulties, help say, "Who is sufficient for these things?" But with simple confidence and trust we may and do say, "Our sufficiency is of God."

Even after her death, Louisa's legacy of faith continued to echo in the African hills of Southern Rhodesia. Her daughter, Lily, remained at the missionary station for many years after her mother's retirement. In addition, a fellow missionary stated that, although she missed Louisa terribly, she never felt far from her because of the five thousand African Christians who continually sang her hymn, "'Tis So Sweet to Trust in Jesus!"

'Tis So Sweet to Trust in Jesus

Louisa M. Stead

William J. Kirkpatrick

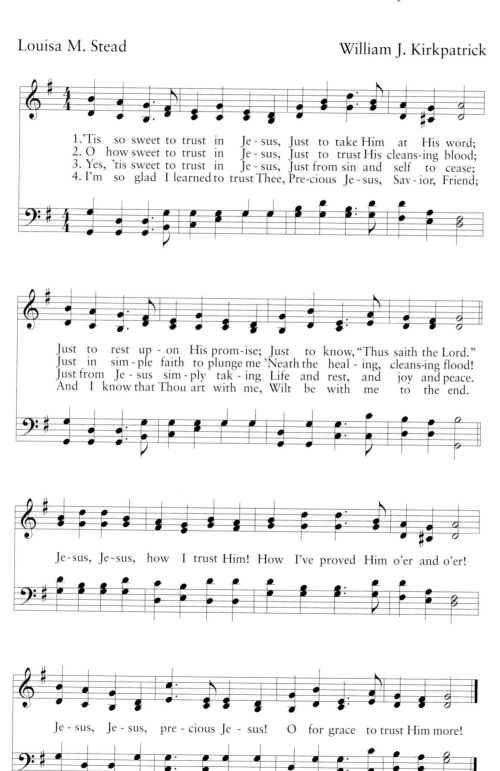

1. 'Tis so sweet to trust in Je - sus, Just to take Him at His word;
2. O how sweet to trust in Je - sus, Just to trust His cleans-ing blood;
3. Yes, 'tis sweet to trust in Je - sus, Just from sin and self to cease;
4. I'm so glad I learned to trust Thee, Pre-cious Je - sus, Sav-ior, Friend;

Just to rest up - on His prom-ise; Just to know, "Thus saith the Lord."
Just in sim - ple faith to plunge me 'Neath the heal - ing, cleans-ing flood!
Just from Je - sus sim - ply tak - ing Life and rest, and joy and peace.
And I know that Thou art with me, Wilt be with me to the end.

Je-sus, Je-sus, how I trust Him! How I've proved Him o'er and o'er!

Je - sus, Je - sus, pre-cious Je - sus! O for grace to trust Him more!

Take My Life, and Let It Be

Frances Ridley Havergal, 1836–1879

BECOMING A LIVING PRAYER

When William Havergal, an influential Anglican clergyman, named his youngest daughter, he sought to give her a legacy. In doing so, he christened her with the middle name of Ridley after Bishop Nicholas Ridley, a famous sixteenth-century English martyr. It would seem a great burden to be laid upon a tiny girl, but Frances Ridley Havergal demonstrated from an early age that her father's aspirations would not be disappointed.

By the time she was three, Frances, or Fanny as she was called, could already read. At the age of four, she moved on from children's literature to the Bible and began not only to read it but also to memorize it. Her prodigious mind appeared insatiable, and at seven she was writing poetry. She quickly learned both Hebrew and Greek and before the age of ten conversed in several modern languages as well. She loved music and became an accomplished pianist and vocalist. It is little wonder the happy and well-adjusted child was nicknamed "Little Quicksilver" by her doting father.

But Fanny's life was not untouched by sorrow. Her beloved mother became seriously ill when the girl was only eleven. Some of her last words would guide Fanny for the rest of her life: "Fanny dear," she whispered earnestly, "pray God to prepare you for all He is preparing for you." Within a few days, Mrs. Havergal was gone, but her words became Frances's guiding principle.

Possessing amazing discipline and remarkable faith for one so young, Frances developed daily habits of prayer and Bible study. As a young teen, she experienced a spiritual conversion and dedicated her life to the praise and worship of God. She reported that, "There and then I committed my soul to the Savior—and earth and heaven seemed brighter from that moment."

Despite the brightness of her spirit, Frances's late teens were darkened by unhappiness. Her father remarried and she did not get along well with her stepmother. When she was eighteen, she contracted an illness that lasted for nine years. But like many spiritually powerful individuals, Frances's ministry seemed to blossom after her time in the "wilderness."

Combining her gifts of writing and music, Frances poured out her love for Christ in verses and songs. She once said:

> Writing hymns is like praying, for I never seem to write even a verse by myself. I feel like a child writing. You know a child will look up at every sentence and ask, 'What shall I say next?' That is what I do. Every line and word and rhyme comes from God.

Despite her frequent bouts with illness, Frances enjoyed traveling and visiting with friends. On one occasion, in 1874, she, along with several others, was spending a few days at the home of a friend. As she became acquainted with the other visitors, she felt burdened for their spiritual condition. In prayer she begged the Lord to "give me all in this house." In a testimony to Frances's faith and the Lord's providence, her prayer was answered, as each of the guests experienced a spiritual renewal. The night before her departure, Frances was too excited and joyful to sleep. In the midst of her own personal revival, the words to a poem of rededication flowed from her pen.

The hymn would be known as "Take My Life, and Let It Be"—a testimony to the driving force in the life of this frail English woman. Four years after penning this poem, Frances determined to fulfill the first words in the fourth verse: "Take my silver and my gold, not a mite would I withhold." She packed up her personal heirloom jewelry collection of over fifty pieces and sent it off to the church missionary society to help finance a Bible teaching ministry for women in India. She told friends she had never packed a box with so much pleasure.

In 1879, at the age of forty-two, Frances learned she didn't have long to live and declared that this news was "too good to be true!" When the time came for her to join her beloved Savior, Frances softly raised her voice in song one last time with the words of one of her own hymns, "Golden Harps Are Sounding."

Frances Ridley Havergal was small in stature, lived only four decades, and never traveled across the ocean; but her hymns of praise to Jesus have circled the globe and given hope to millions of believers in the century since her passing.

Take My Life, and Let It Be

Frances R. Havergal

William B. Bradbury

1. Take my life, and let it be Con - se - crat-ed, Lord, to thee;
2. Take my feet, and let them be Swift and beau - ti - ful for thee;
3. Take my sil - ver and my gold, Not a mite would I with-hold;
4. Take my will, and make it thine, It shall be no long - er mine;

Take my hands and let them move At the im-pulse of thy love.
Take my voice and let me sing Al - ways, on - ly, for my King.
Take my mo-ments and my days, Let them flow in cease-less praise.
Take my heart, it is thine own, It shall be thy roy-al throne.

Lord, I give my life to thee, Thine for - ev - er-more to be;

Lord, I give my life to thee, Thine for - ev-er-more to be.

Jesus Loves Me
Anna Bartlett Warner, 1820—1915

A TALE OF TWO SISTERS

Sometimes the simplest of statements can have a very profound impact, even upon the most sophisticated people. Such is the case with this well-loved children's song. In fact, when the respected Swiss theologian Karl Barth was asked by an interviewer to share the most important discovery he had made in all his years of theological study, he replied: "Jesus loves me! This I know, for the Bible tells me so."

The source of Barth's affirmation was not in a treatise on theology but in a best-selling novel written as a collaboration by two sisters. Anna and Susan Warner were born in New York City to a well-known and prosperous attorney. Summers were spent at the family vacation home, called Good Crag, located on Constitution Island, an island in the Hudson River near the United States Military Academy at West Point. After losing heavily in the panic of 1837, Warner had to give up his house in the city, and Good Crag became the family residence. The move to this more rural environment appeared to spark the sisters' interest in publishing. Both Anna and Susan were devout Christians, highly educated, and gifted writers. From an early age, they composed poetry, short stories, and, eventually, full-length novels. Now, with their financial reversal, they realized they could contribute to the family's security by publishing their work.

It was in the course of writing one of their novels that the words to this favorite hymn were penned. The book actually bears Susan Warner's name as author, but it is Anna who is given credit for the verse, "Jesus Loves Me." In the novel, *Say and Seal*, two of the main characters, Faith Derrick and John Linden, befriend a little boy named Johnny Fax. Johnny becomes very ill, and as his condition worsens, Faith and John decide to pay him a visit. During the course of this visit it becomes clear that little Johnny is near death. Feverish and in pain, the boy asks John Linden, his Sunday school teacher, to hold him. Picking up the dying child, Linden tenderly carries him in his arms as he walks slowly back and forth across the room. Mustering a bit of strength, Johnny cries out, "Sing!" and in an effort to console the child the teacher sings the simple and beautiful words written by Anna Warner:

> Jesus loves me! This I know,
> For the Bible tells me so,
> Little ones to Him belong,
> They are weak, but He is strong.

Within a few hours, Johnny Fax passes into the arms of the Savior who loves him so.

Although *Say and Seal* had a limited life as a popular novel, the four-line poem sung by the fictitious Sunday school teacher went on to become one of the best-loved and most-often sung hymns in the world. It was the famous composer William Bradbury who set the words to music in 1861 and added the two-line chorus, "Yes, Jesus loves me!/Yes, Jesus loves me!/Yes, Jesus loves me!/The Bible tells me so."

At the death of their father, the two sisters were left with little more than their house and land, and they relied upon their writing as their sole source of income. Anna and Susan Warner went on to write several serious literary works, as well as additional novels. One of Susan's books, *The Wide, Wide World*, even became a best seller in the latter part of the nineteenth century, second only to *Uncle Tom's Cabin* by Harriet Beecher Stowe. Anna composed novels under the pen name of Amy Lothrop, as well as several collections of hymn poems under her own name.

In addition to their writing, the two Warner women devoted many hours to teaching Bible classes for the West Point Cadets at the U.S. Military Academy. Upon their deaths, their beloved home, Good Crag, was willed to the Academy; and today, because of the island's history, the home is a national shrine. As a testament to their spiritual contributions to the lives of the young cadets, both Anna and Susan were buried with full military honors.

Their hymn "Jesus Loves Me" has become one of the best-loved Christian songs of all time. Missionaries from around the world have used this clear and simple message of Christian love to minister to their congregations. Its simple eloquence speaks to the child within us all who longs to be comforted with the assurance that Jesus really does love us.

Jesus Loves Me

Anna B. Warner

William B. Bradbury

1. Je-sus loves me! this I know, For the Bi-ble tells me so;
2. Je-sus loves me! he who died Heav-en's gates to o-pen wide!
3. Je-sus loves me! loves me still, Tho I'm ver-y weak and ill;
4. Je-sus loves me! he will stay Close be-side me all the way;

Lit-tle ones to him be-long; They are weak, but he is strong.
He will wash a-way my sin, Let his lit-tle child come in.
From his shin-ing throne on high, Comes to watch me where I lie.
If I love him, when I die He will take me home on high.

Yes, Je-sus loves me, Yes, Je-sus loves me,

Yes, Je-sus loves me, The Bi-ble tells me so.

Jesus, the Very Thought of Thee

Bernard of Clairvaux, 1091–1153

OUT OF THE DARKNESS, LIGHT

The close of the first millennium A.D. was a time of great darkness for the church. Corruption was rampant in the institution founded to protect and preserve the beauty and purity of Christ. Many of the leaders who called themselves Christians behaved in ways that betrayed every one of the Lord's instructions to His followers; yet in the midst of this time that history has called the "Dark Ages," there were some people who truly and devoutly worshiped Christ. Such were the parents of Bernard of Clairvaux.

In the year of 1091, Bernard was born in the town of Fontaine in Burgundy, France. His father was a Burgundian knight, and his mother was a noblewoman known for her grace, virtue, and devotion to God. Together they trained their young son in the graceful manners, high ideals, and Christian values they espoused. Bernard was an eager student. At an early age he demonstrated unusual piety and scholarship. His parents may have believed that their son would follow in the footsteps of his father; yet when his mother died, it was her life of holy devotion that he sought to emulate.

Shortly after her death, Bernard decided to enter the monastery of Citeaux. Even at this point in his life, Bernard's leadership and engaging personality were evident as he persuaded twelve of his friends and relatives to join him in his vocation. After three years at Citeaux, the monks asked Brother Bernard to establish other monastic communities throughout Europe. Eager to spread his enthusiasm for God, Bernard accepted the challenge; and at the age of twenty-four, he established the first of 162 additional branches of his monastic order. This first monastery he called *Clara Vallis,* which means beautiful valley. Later the name would be shortened to Clairvaux. Bernard would eventually become its abbot and assume the title Bernard of Clairvaux.

Although situated in a lovely valley, the monastery was far from peaceful. During the construction of the building, bands of robbers constantly terrorized the monks, cut off food and supplies to the small community, and threatened them with starvation. Despite the hardships, Bernard and his companions continued faithfully to minister to the residents of the surrounding areas, teach the Scriptures, study the Bible, and write. His mind was quick, his pen eloquent, and his spiritual insight remarkable. Before long he had attracted pupils from some of the most influential families in France. Kings, prelates, and noblemen came to Clairvaux to seek his counsel; and in 1146, the Pope commissioned him to lead a crusade. So powerful was Bernard's preaching that, as a result of this crusade, thousands were won to the cause of Christ and unashamedly carried the cross as a symbol of their conversion.

With the conclusion of the crusade, Bernard settled once more at Clairvaux and devoted himself to his favorite pursuits—teaching, studying, and writing. In the course of his career as a monk, he wrote books on the monastic life, church government, and the lifestyle of the pious disciples of Christ. In addition to his skill at writing prose, he also had a gift for composing poetry.

In the nineteenth century, Edward Caswall, one of the best-known English translators of his day, used Bernard's poem "Dulcis Jesu Memorial," a 192-line composition on the name of Jesus, as the source of the lines we know as the hymn "Jesus, the Very Thought of Thee." The eloquent theology of these verses has inspired Christians throughout the past two centuries, none more than the famous Scottish missionary David Livingstone, who wrote, "That hymn of St. Bernard on the name of Jesus . . . rings in my ears as I wander across the wide, wide wilderness."

In the more than eight centuries since his death, Bernard's influence has been felt in congregations throughout the world. His writing inspired Martin Luther, who called him "the best monk that ever lived, whom I admire beyond all the rest put together." And his mystical poetry has produced other magnificent hymns, including "Jesus, Thou Joy of Loving Hearts" and "O Sacred Head, Now Wounded." The latter so influenced Johann Sebastian Bach that it has often been called the composer's theme song.

Bernard of Clairvaux was born in a dark moment of history, but the brilliance of his intellect and spiritual insight still shines in our churches and choir lofts whenever his beautiful poetry is sung in praise to Christ.

Jesus, the Very Thought of Thee

Bernard of Clairvaux

John B. Dykes

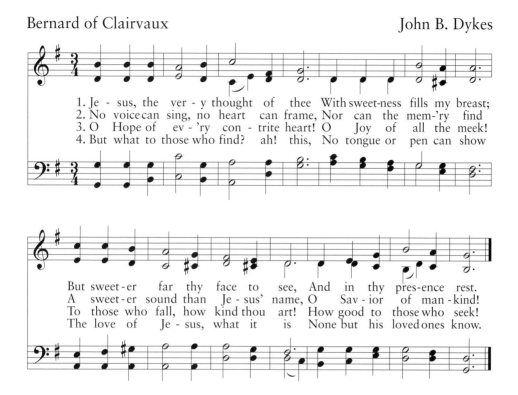

1. Je - sus, the ver - y thought of thee With sweet-ness fills my breast;
2. No voice can sing, no heart can frame, Nor can the mem'ry find
3. O Hope of ev - 'ry con - trite heart! O Joy of all the meek!
4. But what to those who find? ah! this, No tongue or pen can show

But sweet - er far thy face to see, And in thy pres-ence rest.
A sweet - er sound than Je - sus' name, O Sav - ior of man - kind!
To those who fall, how kind thou art! How good to those who seek!
The love of Je - sus, what it is None but his loved ones know.

*Come unto me, all ye that labour
and are heavy laden, and I will give you rest.
Take my yoke upon you, and learn of me;
for I am meek and lowly in heart:
and ye shall find rest unto your souls.
For my yoke is easy,
and my burden is light. Matthew 11:28-30*

Beneath the Cross of Jesus
Elizabeth Clephane, 1830–1869

FOLLOWING THE CROSS

The cross is the enduring symbol of the Christian faith. Emblazoned on banners during the Crusades, lifted high atop cathedrals, worn around the necks of clergy and lay persons, it symbolizes the core value of the believer: the power of sacrificial love. To a young, nineteenth-century Scottish Presbyterian woman, the cross was more than just a symbol. It was her life.

Elizabeth Cecilia Douglas Clephane was born and raised in the beautiful Abbotsford area of Scotland. Elizabeth and her two sisters grew up in a happy home, loved and encouraged by their parents. Although she was known as the quiet and sensitive sister, she had a vivid imagination, an artistic spirit, and an inquisitive mind. She excelled in her schoolwork and loved both reading and writing.

While she was still quite young, Elizabeth's parents both died, leaving the girls in the care of relatives. Instead of succumbing to grief and despair, Elizabeth became even more determined to make her life count for God. It was as though the loss of both her mother and her father heightened the already sensitive girl's compassion and empathy for others. Even though she was plagued by poor health and a delicate constitution, young Miss Clephane devoted hours each day to caring for the sick in her community and providing food and clothing to the poor.

She was an avid student of the Bible and took seriously the words of Christ. When He said, "Whoever will come after me, let him deny himself and take up his cross and follow me," (Matthew 16:24), Elizabeth took it as a personal charge from her Lord. In obedience, she and her sister sold almost all of their belongings, including their horse and carriage, and gave the proceeds to charity. Wherever she went, she shared a cheerful smile and a word of encouragement to those struggling with sickness and poverty. She refused to dwell upon her own suffering and was so encouraging to others that, throughout her hometown of Melrose, she became known as "the sunbeam."

As a child, Elizabeth loved reading and writing; and as an adult, she developed a talent for composing poetry. Most of her poems centered upon religious themes and drew their imagery from both the Old and New Testaments. Although she sent some of her poetry to the Scottish Presbyterian magazine, *The Family Treasury*, most of it was published anonymously, in keeping with the author's desire to give glory only to God. It wasn't until after her death in 1869 at the age of thirty-nine that a larger collection of Elizabeth's poetry was compiled and published.

In this collection were two poems that would become famous hymns. The first was "The Ninety and Nine." In this verse, the author reflects upon Luke 15:3–7, which describes the tender love of the Good Shepherd for His lost sheep. Written originally for children, the verses were first used as a hymn in an evangelistic meeting in Edinburgh by the famous nineteenth-century preacher Dwight L. Moody. His colleague, songwriter Ira Sankey, had read the verses in a Glasgow newspaper only the day before and composed the music at the end of one of their meetings.

The second poem, "Beneath the Cross of Jesus," was set to music by British organist Frederick Charles Maker. Although Elizabeth Clephane, the humble "sunbeam" of Melrose, Scotland, died without ever hearing one of her hymn poems sung, multitudes have been moved to deeper faith by the beauty and eloquence of the biblical imagery in "Beneath the Cross of Jesus." In the first verse, Clephane focuses upon the cross as "the shadow of a mighty rock" (Isaiah 32:2) which provides a "home within the wilderness" (Jeremiah 9:2) and "rest upon the way" (Isaiah 28:12) for those who experience the "burning of the noon-tide heat" (Isaiah 4:6) "and the burden of the day" (Matthew 11:30). The second verse is more of a personal testimony that praises the sacrificial love of Jesus on her behalf. In the third verse Elizabeth's life commitment is stated with clarity and joy. The young woman who shared the sunshine of her faith with those in her community affirms that her only goal is to bask in the sunshine of her Savior's face. Elizabeth Clephane received no earthly glory or praise from the publication of her work, but one cannot help but imagine that the far-reaching effects of her words have earned her the highest praise she could desire: her Savior's "well done."

Beneath the Cross of Jesus

Elizabeth C. Clephane

Frederick C. Maker

1. Be - neath the cross of Je - sus I fain would take my stand,
2. Up - on that cross of Je - sus Mine eye at times can see
3. I take, O cross, thy shad - ow For my a - bid - ing place;

The shad-ow of a might - y rock With - in a wea - ry land;
The ver - y dy - ing form of One Who suf-fered there for me;
I ask no oth - er sun-shine than The sun-shine of His face;

A home with-in the wil - der-ness, A rest up - on the way,
And from my smit-ten heart with tears Two won - ders I con - fess,
Con - tent to let the world go by, To know no gain or loss,

From the burn-ing of the noon-tide heat, And the bur-den of the day.
The won-ders of His glo-rious love And my un-wor-thi - ness.
My sin - ful self my on - ly shame, My glo-ry all the cross.

My Redeemer
Philip P. Bliss 1838–1876

REDEEMED FROM THE FIRE

Born to a poor family in Rome, Pennsylvania, in the summer of 1838, Philip Bliss didn't appear to have many opportunities. Most of his days were spent doing farm work or laboring in a lumber camp. There wasn't much encouragement for "book learning" other than the most basic reading, writing, and arithmetic skills. When young Philip demonstrated a natural gift for music, there was certainly no money to spare for lessons. But along with his musical talents, Philip demonstrated a great determination and spent countless hours studying and learning about music. His heart was drawn to the Scriptures; and by the time he reached his twenties, he was not only writing hymn poems, but also composing melodies.

Raised in poverty, Philip realized he might be able to turn his gift into a profession and escape the economic fate of his friends and family. He learned of a Chicago music publisher; and in 1863, at the age of twenty-five, he sent them a copy of his first music manuscript. Philip included a letter with the manuscript requesting that, if the song were good enough to be published, he be paid not in money but with a flute. After examining the music sent by Bliss, the publisher not only sent him a flute but also encouraged the young musician to submit additional compositions.

Within a year, Philip Bliss had been offered a position with the music publisher; and he packed up his family and moved to Chicago. He immediately began to demonstrate his skills in teaching as well as composing. Soon, Bliss was traveling throughout the Midwest, conducting music conventions and training institutes, leading singing classes, and even performing in evangelical services. All the while, he continued to write what would come to be known as gospel songs. This style of sacred song, different from the classical hymns of previous eras, was known for its strong ties to Scripture and its folksy, easily-sung tunes.

In the summer of 1869, Philip Bliss became acquainted with the noted American evangelist Dwight L. Moody. Moody's meetings were attended by thousands of people seeking a spiritual experience, and the preacher recognized the power of music to reach the soul. Though not a singer himself, Moody sought out those who had the gift of leading others in the singing of sacred music. Providentially, he was introduced to Philip Bliss; and before long, Bliss was leading songs and singing solos in Moody's meetings.

Whatever his other obligations, Philip Bliss continued to turn out new songs at a prodigious rate. Sometimes he would hear a particularly inspiring Scripture verse or sermon illustration at a meeting, go home, and return the next day with a completed song. By 1874 he had compiled a collection of his own works and published them under the title *Gospel Songs*. Some of his more familiar titles are, "Let the Lower Lights Be Burning," "Jesus Loves Even Me," "Hallelujah, What a Savior," and "Wonderful Words of Life." He then began collaborating with Ira D. Sankey. They would have had a long and prolific partnership had tragedy not intervened.

It was the Christmas season of 1876, and Philip and his wife Lucy had just completed a holiday visit with his mother in Rome, Pennsylvania. On December 29, as the train in which they were riding crossed a bridge near Ashtabula, Ohio, the trestle gave way. The railroad cars plunged into the icy waters of the river. Only a few of the 160 passengers survived the initial impact and many of those drowned in the moments after the crash. Amazingly, Philip Bliss was among the survivors and managed to escape through a broken window. Immediately after his escape, however, the wreckage burst into flames. Unable to locate his wife, Bliss returned to the blazing train in hopes of rescuing her. Sadly, neither Philip nor Lucy survived.

In the salvage efforts after the disaster, crews pulled luggage and personal effects from the twisted and charred ruins. In a trunk belonging to Philip Bliss, a manuscript for a new gospel song was discovered. It was the text for "My Redeemer." In the verses, Bliss describes how the love of Jesus, his Redeemer, rescued him from death and brought him to life eternal. They were fitting and prophetic words with which to conclude the career of one of the nineteenth century's most famous gospel songwriters. Although he only lived for thirty-eight years, Philip Bliss blessed the world with his words and melodies and contributed a unique and memorable chapter to the history of sacred music.

My Redeemer

Philip P. Bliss

James McGranahan

1. I will sing of my Re-deem-er, And His won-drous love to me;
2. I will tell the won-drous sto-ry, How my lost es-tate to save,
3. I will praise my dear Re-deem-er, His tri-um-phant power I'll tell,
4. I will sing of my Re-deem-er, And His heav'n-ly love to me;

On the cru-el cross He suf-fered, From the curse to set me free.
In His bound-less love and mer-cy, He the ran-som free-ly gave.
How the vic-to-ry He giv-eth O-ver sin, and death, and hell.
He from death to life hath brought me, Son of God, with Him to be.

Sing, oh, sing of my Re-deem-er,

sing of my Re-deem-er, Sing, oh, sing of my Re-deem-er,

With His blood He pur-chased me,

He pur-chased me, With His blood He pur-chased me,

My

Redeemer

On the cross   He sealed my par - don,
      He sealed my par-don, On the cross He sealed my par-don,

Paid the debt   and made me free.
      and made me free,   and made me free.

Count Your Blessings

Johnson Oatman Jr. 1856–1922

DETERMINED TO BLESS

For some individuals, the road to their goal in life is clearly before them. But for many, including Johnson Oatman Jr., the goal is clear, yet the road seems blocked by obstacles and detours.

Johnson Oatman Jr. was born on April 21, 1856, in the small town of Lumbertown, New Jersey. His father was a businessman who enjoyed singing Christian music and, whenever possible, performing in church services and at evangelical meetings. At one point, he was even proclaimed the best singer in New Jersey. From a young age, Johnson accompanied his father to his singing engagements and listened to the inspirational singing and the stirring messages that often followed. A strong desire grew within the young boy to become a faithful follower of God and a blessing to others—just like his dad.

But young Johnson was not blessed with his father's voice, and it soon became evident that it was unlikely he could pursue a career in vocal music. After graduation from high school, Oatman took a job with his father's mercantile business; but the desire to be a blessing to God continued to burn in his heart. At nineteen, he joined the Methodist Church and became active in its affairs. He didn't find the fulfillment of his dreams in this capacity, however, and wondered if he were called to be a minister of the gospel. Perhaps this was the route to being a blessing. Lacking the resources to attend a seminary, Johnson Oatman Jr. studied on his own and eventually applied for and was granted a ministerial license. Thus prepared, he was able to write and deliver sermons in local congregations.

Feeling confined by the restraints of preaching in just one or two pulpits, Oatman sought out opportunities to speak in a variety of churches. Before long, he had established a regular preaching circuit and offered to speak wherever opportunity allowed. By the time he was in his thirties he had left the family firm for a position with a large New Jersey insurance company, but he still found time to prepare and deliver sermons for his congregations.

Johnson Oatman Jr., however, was still not convinced that he had achieved his life's goal of being a blessing to God and others. In 1888, at the age of thirty-two, he combined his talent for writing sermons with his love of Christian music and began to set down verses of poetry to be used as sacred songs. At last it appeared that Oatman had found his purpose. The verses fairly flew from his pen, and it became clear from the outset that he had an amazing gift for capturing the gospel message in verse. He might not be able to sing like his father or preach like some of the powerful evangelists of his day, but Johnson Oatman Jr. could certainly write inspiring gospel songs. His style was unpretentious and touched a chord with the common people in the pews. His language was clear and unencumbered by heavy imagery. When his hymn poems were set to music, they often became instant favorites. Throughout his lifetime, Oatman would pen over five thousand hymns. It is said that at times he produced them at the rate of four or five a week, all while holding down his administrative job.

It would seem that Oatman's goal of being a blessing was finally accomplished with the composition of his most famous song, "Count Your Blessings." Written in 1897, the poem was set to music by Edwin O. Excell, a composer from Ohio, and was published that same year in a book entitled *Songs for Young People*.

"Count Your Blessings" became an immediate hit on the revival circuit in the United States. The song provided a bright and upbeat reminder of the presence of God in the everyday lives of His people. One minister attested to the song's ability to touch lives by declaring: "Men sing it, boys whistle it and women rock their babies to sleep with it." Thousands were blessed by the encouraging message of Johnson Oatman's words.

It might have taken a long time for Oatman to achieve his goal, but he never gave up. And the words to this famous hymn seem to echo his own life message. Refusing to give in to discouragement, Johnson Oatman Jr. continued to count on and enjoy the blessings of God. He used both the gifts and opportunities provided to him, and in the end it may have even surprised him to see what the Lord had done.

Count Your Blessings

Johnson Oatman Jr.   Edwin O. Excell

1. When up-on life's bil-lows you are tem-pest tossed, When you are dis-
2. Are you ev-er bur-dened with a load of care? Does the cross seem
3. So a-mid the con-flict, wheth-er great or small, Do not be dis-

cour-aged, think-ing all is lost, Count your man-y bless-ings– name them
heav-y you are called to bear? Count your man-y bless-ings; ev-'ry
cour-aged; God is o-ver all. Count your man-y bless-ings; an-gels

one by one, And it will sur-prise you what the Lord hath done.
doubt will fly, And you will be sing-ing as the days go by.
will at-tend, Help and com-fort give you to your jour-ney's end.

Count your bless-ings, name them one by one; Count your
Count your man-y bless-ings, name them one by one; Count your man-y

bless-ings, see what God hath done. Count your bless-ings,
bless-ings, see what God hath done. Count your man-y bless-ings,

51

Count
Your
Blessings

name them one by one;   Count your man-y bless-ings, see what God hath done.

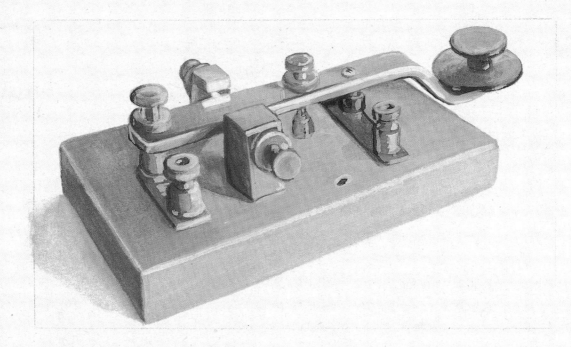

O Master, Let Me Walk with Thee
Washington Gladden, 1836–1918

WALKING THE TALK

The Civil War had ended and the United States was in the midst of a new revolution. Industry was thriving, businesses were booming, and there was money to be made in the rebirth of the nation. But all the economic promise had a darker side as well. The growth of industry required a multitude of cheap workers, and the poor were exploited in order to feed the nation's hunger for new products. Progress had its price and Washington Gladden felt it was way too high.

Born in February of 1836, Gladden was raised on a farm in Potts Grove, Pennsylvania. After high school, he attended Williams College and graduated in 1859. Shortly thereafter, he received his ordination from the Congregational Church and began a ministry that was as effective as it was controversial. Washington Gladden refused to steer clear of divisive issues and used his position not only to preach the gospel as a spiritual guide but also as a call to social action. Traveling and speaking from Congregational pulpits up and down the East Coast, Gladden angered business leaders and political groups with his charges that they exploited workers for "economic progress." Through Gladden's editorials in the *New York Independent,* he exposed the illegal practices of politicians who worked to control the laws for personal gain. Washington Gladden was a thorn in the flesh of the establishment; but his outspoken criticism was not limited to the secular world.

Some of his harshest diatribes were reserved for the Christian community. He, along with other socially active clergy of the day, such as the English evangelist William Booth, founder of the Salvation Army, believed that the church needed to lead, not follow, the fight for social justice. Gladden wrote that it was the duty of the Christian church and its leaders to "elevate the masses not only spiritually and morally, but to be concerned about their social and economic welfare as well." His powerful efforts on behalf of those he viewed as exploited brought more than a little controversy his way. But Gladden was not afraid to take on some of the most powerful individuals in the country.

When John D. Rockefeller Sr. generously donated $100,000 to the Foreign Mission Board of the Congregational Church, Gladden urged the church to turn down the money. He feared the money might be ill-gotten gains because of the oil monopoly of Rockefeller. On the religious front, Gladden angered just about the entire conservative wing of Christianity with his declaration that the Bible should be viewed solely as a book on religion and not as an inerrant source on matters of science and history. Despite his often abrasive and sometimes unorthodox opinions, Washington Gladden became one of the most powerful and respected members of the social-gospel movement in the country.

In 1882, at the age of forty-six, Gladden was called to be the pastor of the First Congregational Church in Columbus, Ohio. He would remain there for the next thirty-two years. But his move away from the East Coast did nothing to dilute his passion for social justice. He was instrumental in arbitrating strikes since he was renowned for his negotiating skills and driven by his deep convictions.

Those convictions emerged in his sermons, speeches, editorials, and letters, but today Washington Gladden is usually not remembered for any of those. Instead, he is more familiar as the writer of a single hymn—a hymn that was never intended to be sung at all. As one means of conveying his ideas and championing his cause, Gladden edited a publication entitled *Sunday Afternoon*. In one issue, Gladden published a devotional poem he entitled "Walking With God." The original poem had six verses and spoke of the writer's desire to walk with God in such a way as to bring inspiration, hope, peace, and courage to those who struggled to live their faith in daily experiences. When it was suggested to Gladden that he consider setting the poem to music, he chose an existing melody by Anglican minister H. Percy Smith. In 1879, "O Master, Let Me Walk with Thee" was first published as a hymn. The clarity of Gladden's call to social action still rings in the words of his hymn; and wherever it is sung, Christians are challenged to live out their faith not just in words but also in deeds.

O Master, Let Me Walk with Thee

Washington Gladden   H. Percy Smith

1. O Master, let me walk with Thee In lowly paths of service free; Tell me Thy secret, help me bear The strain of toil, the fret of care.

2. Help me the slow of heart to move By some clear, winning word of love; Teach me the wayward feet to stay, And guide them in the homeward way.

3. Teach me Thy patience; still with Thee In closer, dearer company, In work that keeps faith sweet and strong, In trust that triumphs over wrong.

4. In hope that sends a shining ray Far down the future's broad'ning way, In peace that only Thou canst give, With Thee, O Master, let me live.

He hath shewed thee, O man, what is good;
and what doth the Lord require of thee,
but to do justly, and to love mercy,
and to walk humbly with thy God? Micah 6:8

I Love to Tell the Story

Katherine Hankey, 1834–1911

A STORY TO TELL

By the middle of the nineteenth century, the evangelical movement, begun in rural England by George Whitefield and John and Charles Wesley a century earlier, had gripped the influential political and business leaders of London. Within the Anglican Church a group of wealthy evangelical philanthropists formed a group called the Clapham Sect, named after the exclusive Clapham district of southwest London. Led by William Wilberforce, the members of this group shared a common passion for applying the gospel of Christ to all aspects of society. They campaigned zealously against the slave trade throughout the British Empire and sought ways to improve the plight of the poor and destitute working in the factories and sweatshops of London. In addition, they worked to influence legislation that would use Christian ethics as a basis for defining policies of social, political, national, and international affairs.

In 1834, Katherine Hankey was born into the family of one of the members of this Clapham Sect. Kate, as she was known, grew up hearing her father, a wealthy London banker, and his friends debate the importance of the Church's role in social matters. These zealous laypeople not only spoke about their concerns but also devoted large portions of their time and money to supporting programs that improved the lot of thousands of English citizens in the name of Christ.

No doubt influenced by her father and his associates, Kate determined to reach out to those less fortunate than she. As a teenager she taught Bible classes. Later she wrote and taught lessons based on Scripture to her wealthy friends, as well as to the young women who worked in the factories. Her gifts for writing, teaching, and preaching were rewarded by a large number of enthusiastic students who, following her lead, became Christian workers themselves.

But Kate Hankey is not remembered for her Christian social activism as much as for two hymns she wrote. They were composed when she was thirty years old, while convalescing from a serious illness. Prior to her illness, Kate had enjoyed writing Bible lessons, teaching church doctrine, and composing religious poetry. Despite her physical discomfort, she determined to compose a lengthy poem based on the life of Christ. When completed, the poem consisted of two sections, each fifty verses in length. The first was entitled "The Story Wanted" and the second, "The Story Told." The text for the hymn, "Tell Me the Old, Old Story," came from the first section of this poem and from the second came the text for "I Love to Tell the Story." Both hymns were initially sung to a tune also composed by Hankey.

The hymns did not reach popularity, however, until the following year. Major General Russell, commander of English forces, was a featured speaker at an international convention of the YMCA held in Montreal, Canada, in 1867. When he took the podium, he softly said, " I merely want to read a very beautiful poem which should be the dominant theme undergirding everything we do here." With that, Russell read the texts of Miss Hankey's two hymns. In the audience that evening was Dr. William Howard Doane, an American inventor and composer. Dr. Doane later reported, "So impressed was I with the words that I requested a copy. Later, when travelling [home] I composed a tune for the words and added a simple little chorus." A few years later, a new melody and ending refrain was written for "I Love to Tell the Story" by another American, William G. Fischer. It was in this form that Katherine Hankey's hymn was included in the popular collection, *Gospel Hymns and Sacred Songs* in 1875. Popularized in international evangelical meetings by Ira Sankey, the hymn soon became a favorite wherever it was sung.

Katherine recovered from her illness and went on to minister through her writing and teaching for four more decades. A trip to South Africa to bring home her invalid brother ignited her interest in international ministries, and she made a commitment to donate all her writing income to foreign missions. In her own community, she spent her last years sharing her hopeful message with the sick and lonely patients confined to London's hospitals. It is not difficult to imagine this dear English saint as she traveled from bedside to bedside tenderly telling each one she encountered "the old, old story of Jesus and His love."

I Love to Tell the Story

Katherine Hankey   William G. Fischer

1. I love to tell the sto-ry Of un-seen things a-bove, Of
3. I love to tell the sto-ry, 'Tis pleas-ant to re-peat What
3. I love to tell the sto-ry, For those who know it best Seem

Je-sus and His glo-ry, Of Je-sus and His love. I love to
seems each time I tell it, More won-der-ful-ly sweet. I love to
hun-ger-ing and thirst-ing To hear it like the rest. And when, in

tell the sto-ry, Be-cause I know 'tis true; It sat-is-fies my
tell the sto-ry, For some have nev-er heard The mes-age of sal-
scenes of glo-ry, I sing the new, new song, 'Twill be the old, old

long-ings As noth-ing else can do.
va-tion From God's own ho-ly Word. I love to tell the sto-ry, 'Twill
sto-ry That I have loved so long.

be my theme in glo-ry To tell the old, old sto-ry of Je-sus and His love.

Still, Still with Thee

Harriet Beecher Stowe, 1812–1896

RESTING IN GOD

Harriet Beecher Stowe is most often remembered as the author of the best-selling novel *Uncle Tom's Cabin,* but she also wrote over three dozen other books, including a volume of religious poetry. Given her family background, some might say it was inevitable that she become such a famous and prolific writer.

Harriet was born on June 14, 1812, in Litchfield, Connecticut. Her father, Dr. Lyman Beecher, was regarded as the most powerful American Puritan preacher of his generation. He was said to have been greatly influenced by the fiery eighteenth-century theologian and preacher, Jonathan Edwards. Her mother was a devout Christian who died when Harriet was only three years old. Although without a mother, the little girl was loved by her father, six brothers, and sister. By the time she was six, she could read and had memorized over two dozen hymns and two entire chapters from the Bible. She and her siblings received their formal education at a private school where her father taught the Bible. The success of the Beecher children should attest to the excellence of their education: Harriet's youngest brother would one day outshine his father as the nation's most famous preacher, Henry Ward Beecher. Her sister, Catherine, would found her own school. And Harriet would go on to write a novel that would become a worldwide bestseller.

The background for that novel came from the convictions that Harriet developed after moving with her family to Cincinnati, Ohio, when she was twenty-two. Her family was actively involved in helping slaves escape to Canada through the underground railroad. Her encounters with these fugitives reinforced her abolitionist leanings and validated her beliefs that Christians should never tolerate the mistreatment of others.

Harriet lived with her family in Cincinnati until 1836, when she married Dr. Calvin Stowe, a professor and Bible authority teaching at Lane. They moved to Maine, where her husband took a position at the Andover Theological Seminary. The Stowes eventually had six children and Harriet took on the responsibility of raising them, as her husband suffered from poor health. At times, his illness required him to be confined to a sanatorium, and Harriet's responsibilities became even greater. With money in short supply, she began writing articles for magazines to bring in some extra income. The themes of social justice and Christian faith ran through her articles; and, at one point, she was urged by a relative to write something that would "cause the whole nation to feel what an accursed thing slavery is." Overwhelmed with her own personal problems, Harriet promised that she would certainly try to do something in the future. With a houseful of children, her youngest son just a toddler and her husband suffering from depression because of his continual health problems, the young mother couldn't imagine composing a large work. But she was already writing magazine articles and decided to try her hand at a serial piece. The last installment was barely on the newsstands when a Boston publisher approached the author about publishing *Uncle Tom's Cabin* as a book. When it was released in 1852, Harriet Beecher Stowe became one of the most famous women in the world. Her book sold over a million copies in the United States alone and was published overseas in twenty different languages.

Harriet's joy, however, was tempered by the challenges within her own family. Her son Charles was stricken with cholera and died. In her grief, Harriet penned the words of a poem we know as the hymn "Still, Still with Thee," which was eventually set to music composed by Felix Mendelssohn.

The comforting words of her hymn would come back to her in later times of distress. Her eldest son, Henry, drowned at the end of his first year at Dartmouth College, and her third son was wounded at Gettysburg and was left with severe disabilities.

The faith that Harriet Beecher Stowe first professed at the age of thirteen was severely tried; yet throughout her life, she testified to the unwavering sense of God's presence sustaining her. She received accolades from some of the most renowned individuals of her day; and yet one senses that the truth that delighted her more than all her fame was that she could say in confidence to her Savior, "I am still, still with Thee."

Still, Still with Thee

Harriet B. Stowe

Felix Mendelssohn

1. Still, still with Thee, when pur - ple morn - ing break - eth,
2. A - lone with Thee, a - mid the mys - tic shad - ows,
3. Still, still to Thee! as to each new - born morn - ing,
4. So shall it be at last in that bright morn - ing,

When the bird wak - eth, and the shad - ows flee;
The sol - emn hush of na - ture new - ly born;
A fresh and sol - emn splen - dor still is giv'n,
When the soul wak - eth, and life's shad - ows flee;

Fair - er than morn - ing love - li - er than day - light,
A - lone with Thee in breath - less ad - o - ra - tion,
So does this bless - ed con - scious - ness a - wak - ing,
O in that hour, fair - er than day - light dawn - ing,

Dawns the sweet con - scious - ness I am with Thee.
In the calm dew and fresh - ness of the morn.
Breathe each day near - ness un - to Thee and heav'n.
Shall rise the glo - rious tho't I am with Thee.

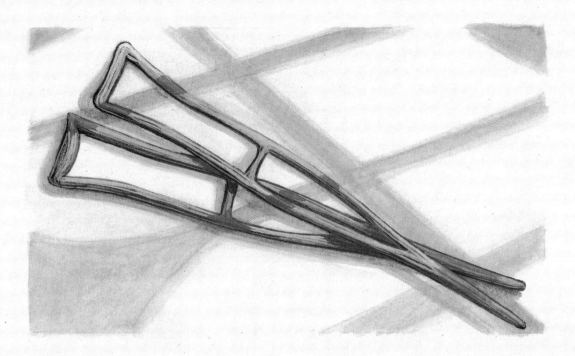

Day by Day
Carolina Sandell Berg, 1832–1903

TRUSTING ONE DAY AT A TIME

Spiritual revivals swept across England and the United States during the nineteenth century, but it is sometimes forgotten that Scandinavia experienced its own series of such revivals as well. In Sweden, a woman named Carolina Sandell contributed over six hundred hymns to the evangelistic movement. Her hymns were known for their heart-warming messages of faith and trust in God, but many who sang them never realized the path the author had traveled in order to write such inspirational verses.

Carolina Sandell, or Lina as she was called, was born on October 3, 1832, in the town of Froderyd, Sweden. She was both frail and very shy and, consequently, spent most of her childhood indoors. Her favorite companions were books, and she spent many hours in her father's study poring over his many volumes of literature and history. Because she did not go to school, her teacher was her father, who tutored her at home. Her father was the pastor of the local parish church, and he passed along his love of the Bible and his methods of studying the Scriptures to his young daughter. By the time she was in her teens, Lina had acquired an excellent liberal arts education and demonstrated a gift for writing. In addition, she had developed a deep and abiding trust in the Lord and a confidence that He would always love and care for her.

When Lina was only twelve, her young faith was severely tested. She became seriously ill and spent many weeks confined to her bed. When she began to recover from her sickness, it was discovered that the disease had left her partially paralyzed. The doctors who examined her finally gave the family the sad news that there was no hope for a recovery and that Lina would never walk again. Although they were grieved by the news, the pastor and his family determined to make Lina's life as normal as possible. But Lina had other ideas. She had read the gospels and the words of Christ to His disciples about having faith and trusting in God in all circumstances. So one day, while her family was at church services, Lina prayed specifically that the Lord would help her to get out of bed and walk. Then in an act of childlike faith, the little girl reached for her clothes, sat up in bed, and began to dress herself. When she was clothed, she swung her legs off the bed, slowly stood up, and began to walk across the room. Her family could hardly believe their eyes when they returned from services to find Lina standing in the parlor.

From that time on, Lina determined to live in gratitude to the Lord who had healed her. Her writing became more reflective of her deep spiritual convictions, and she started keeping a journal of her thoughts and poems. When she was only sixteen, she published her first book, a small volume of poetry.

Lina's faith was to be severely tested again when she was twenty-six. Her father planned a trip to Gothenburg and Lina decided to accompany him. As they crossed Lake Vattern the two of them stood by the boat's railing, admiring the beautiful scenery. Suddenly the boat lurched and Lina's father fell overboard. Lina watched, horrified, as her beloved father drowned.

Heartbroken, Lina returned home. This time her wounds were not merely physical. For almost three years after the tragedy, she experienced a deep sadness of soul. Her family and friends continually prayed for God to lift her despair. As the months passed, the depression lessened and the young woman's faith began to emerge. It would be from this time of soul sickness and recovery that some of Lina's most powerful hymns would be written.

Lina married C.O. Berg, a Stockholm merchant, when she was thirty-five, but she continued to write her hymns and poetry under her maiden name. The popularity of her hymns in Sweden was due, in part, to the melodies written by an associate of Lina's, Oscar Ahnfelt. Ahnfelt was both a composer and singer and was well-known in Scandinavia as the "spiritual troubadour." He traveled from place to place with his ten-string guitar, singing in churches and at evangelical meetings.

Lina Sandell did not have an easy life; but through her difficulties, she recognized that she never had to face her challenges alone. It was this realization she so eloquently expressed in her beautiful hymn "Day by Day." She had learned that, although life was unpredictable, God's love is constant and He alone provides the strength we need for each passing moment.

Day by Day

Carolina V. Sandell Berg   Oscar Ahnfelt

1. Day by day and with each pass-ing mo-ment, Strength I
2. Ev-'ry day the Lord Him-self is near me With a
3. Help me then in ev-'ry trib-u-la-tion So to

find to meet my tri-als here; Trust-ing in my Fa-ther's
spe-cial mer-cy for each hour; All my cares He fain would
trust Your prom-is-es, O Lord, That I lose not faith's sweet

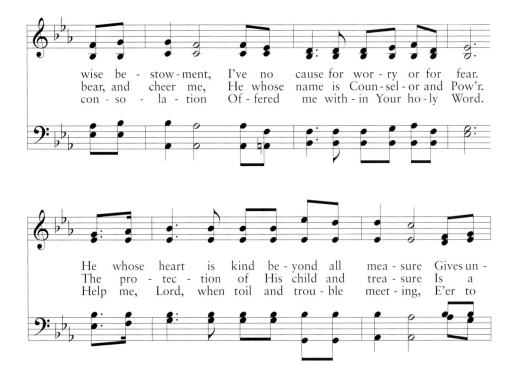

wise be-stow-ment, I've no cause for wor-ry or for fear.
bear, and cheer me, He whose name is Coun-sel-or and Pow'r.
con-so-la-tion Of-fered me with-in Your ho-ly Word.

He whose heart is kind be-yond all mea-sure Gives un-
The pro-tec-tion of His child and trea-sure Is a
Help me, Lord, when toil and trou-ble meet-ing, E'er to

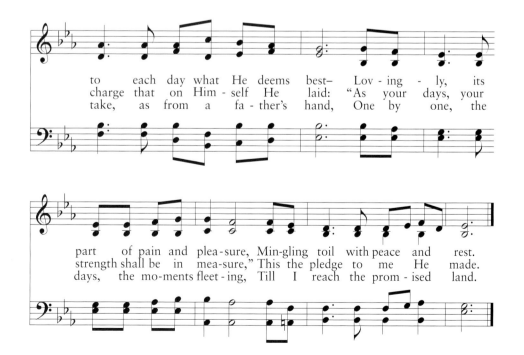

to each day what He deems best— Lov-ing-ly, its
charge that on Him-self He laid: "As your days, your
take, as from a fa-ther's hand, One by one, the

part of pain and plea-sure, Min-gling toil with peace and rest.
strength shall be in mea-sure," This the pledge to me He made.
days, the mo-ments fleet-ing, Till I reach the prom-ised land.

All Glory, Laud, and Honor

Theodulf of Orleans, ?-821 and John M. Neale, 1818-1866

A MASTERPIECE BRIDGING A MILLENNIUM

It is not unusual to find a hymn that is a collaboration between two writers. Often one may write the verse and the other adds a refrain. It is certainly less common, however, to find a hymn that is a collaboration between two individuals who lived more than one thousand years apart. Hymn writer John M. Neale, however, was one who worked almost exclusively with partners who had died centuries, or even a millennium, before he was born.

Theodulf was born in Spain in the eighth century. He was a pious young man and dedicated himself to the religious life. He traveled to France, where he became known and revered as a poet and pastor. In his capacity as a priest, Theodulf became acquainted with Charlemagne, the emperor who saw as his destiny the revival of the ancient Roman Empire. In about 781, Charlemagne summoned Theodulf to his court at Aachen, Germany. There the priest served his emperor as both confessor and confidant. As a reward for his faithful service, Theodulf was appointed bishop of Orleans, France. For more than two decades, the priest dedicated himself to the people of Orleans, where he was known and loved as a pious, yet personable, man of

God. But when Charlemagne died and his son Louis I succeeded him on the throne in 814, the new emperor looked with suspicion upon those who had served his father. The bishop of Orleans was accused of disloyalty and imprisoned in a small cell in his own monastery. Theodulf languished there for seven years. Deprived of companionship, the priest found solace in poetry and prayer. Often, those walking near his cell could hear Theodulf singing his own poetry in earnest tones, apparently offering it to a heavenly audience known only to the lonely priest. On one occasion the emperor visited the monastery where Theodulf was imprisoned. Chancing to pass near the priest's cell, it is recorded that the emperor paused when he heard the prisoner singing, "All glory, laud, and honor/ To Thee, Redeemer, King / To whom the lips of children / Made sweet hosannas ring."

Moved to tears by the words and stricken with guilt that he had imprisoned such a pious man, the emperor ordered the priest released. History records, however, that Theodulf never left the monastery alive; mystery shrouds the bishop's death that occurred shortly after the emperor's visit. But, as it turned out, even death would not silence Theodulf of Orleans.

The words of this godly bishop from the early Middle Ages might never have been discovered had it not been for an unusually diligent nineteenth-century British scholar, John M. Neale. Neale was born in London in 1818 and grew up with a love of languages and literature. After completing his studies at Cambridge University, he was ordained to the ministry of the Church of England. His thirst for learning and his fascination with church history motivated him to study twenty languages and hundreds of ancient religious documents. His reading led him to write volumes defining the early years of the church, ancient architecture, and other esoteric subjects; but the discoveries that would bring Neale his greatest and most lasting fame would be his translations of Medieval Latin hymns. Through his pen, the centuries-old texts were given new life and meter. When set to music and sung by choirs and congregations, their haunting beauty filled cathedrals and churches around the world.

In 1860, John Neale translated the Latin poem written in 820 by Theodulf. Shortly thereafter the words were set to music that had been composed in 1630 by Melchior Teschner, a Lutheran pastor in Germany, and became the classic hymn of praise, "All Glory, Laud, and Honor." Thus, a collaboration that spanned over a thousand years by three men of different denominations and nationalities produced a hymn that is found today in almost every Protestant and Catholic hymnal. It stands as a testimony to the richness of a faith able to bridge cultures, languages, and time in order to offer praises to the God of all.

But thou, O Lord, shalt endure for ever;
and thy remembrance unto all generations. Psalm 102:12

All Glory, Laud, and Honor

Theodulf of Orleans

John M. Neale

1. All glo-ry, laud, and hon - or To Thee, Re-deem-er King,
2. The com-pan - y of an - gels Are prais-ing Thee on high,
3. To Thee, be-fore Thy pas - sion They sang their hymns of praise;

To whom the lips of chil - dren Made sweet ho-san-nas ring.
And mor-tal men and all things Cre - a - ted make re - ply.
To Thee, now high ex-alt - ed, Our mel - o - dy we raise.

Thou art the King of Is - ra - el, Thou Da - vid's roy - al Son,
The peo-ple of the He - brews With palms be - fore Thee went,
Thou didst ac - cept their prais - es; Ac - cept the prayers we bring,

Who in the Lord's name com - est, The King and bless - ed One.
Our praise and prayer and an - thems Be - fore Thee we pre - sent.
Who in all good de - light - est, Thou good and gra-cious King.

Doxology
Thomas Ken, 1637–1711

FAMOUS PRAISES FROM A BOLD BISHOP

During times of change, those with strong wills and bold ideas challenge the established order. Such was the case of Bishop Thomas Ken, a man who was small in stature but larger than life in his influence upon his church and government.

Thomas Ken's early life could have led him to a life of poverty, but Providence determined otherwise. After losing both his parents at an early age, Thomas was rescued from being sent to an orphanage by his older sister, Annie. She and her husband, Izaak Walton, decided to take Thomas into their home and raise him. It was a very fortunate move for young Thomas. His keen mind and strong spirit were challenged by the intellect of his guardian, Izaak Walton, who became famous in England as the author of *The Compleat Angler*. The Waltons raised Thomas to value inquiry and education and sent him to the prestigious Winchester College at Oxford University. Upon his graduation in 1662, he was ordained as a priest in the Church of England. From the outset, however, Thomas Ken brought controversy to his position as a church leader.

He initially served in Winchester, where he was determined to introduce the singing of hymns as part of regular worship in the church. This was a radical idea in the seventeenth century. But radical ideas never bothered Thomas Ken.

In 1679, when the English monarch Charles II was asked to send an English chaplain to the court at The Hague, Ken was selected for the job. Upon his arrival in the Dutch capital, however, the outspoken English priest observed the corruption among the political officials and began denouncing them at every opportunity. Within a year, Thomas Ken was shipped back to his own country.

It appears that the experience did nothing to chasten Ken, because he immediately turned his criticism upon his own monarch. Despite this, Charles II kept the outspoken chaplain at court and appeared to look upon the "good little man" as a sort of external conscience. When it was time for the king to go to chapel services, he would sigh and say to his advisors that he must now "go in and hear Ken tell me my faults." Perhaps he found the truth a rare and refreshing commodity in the midst of the tangled court intrigues.

As a reward for his honesty and courage, King Charles II appointed Thomas Ken as the Bishop of Bath and Wells. Only twelve days after this appointment, however, the king died. When Thomas Ken was commanded to pledge his loyalty to the new monarch, James II, he refused on the grounds that James was a papist. That decision landed the rebellious bishop in the Tower of London. Undaunted, Ken refused to recant. He lost his bishopric, but fortunately was released from the tower and allowed to live out his remaining years in the home of an old friend in the English countryside. In 1711, at the age of seventy-four, the courageous little priest passed away.

According to his own request, his coffin was carried by "six of the poorest men in the parish" and his body was buried "under the east window of the chancel of Frome church at sunrise." As the first rays of sunlight fell upon the churchyard and the casket was lowered into the grave, Thomas Ken's friends sang the hymn he had written over thirty-five years earlier, "Awake, My Soul and with the Sun."

Thomas Ken had penned the hymn while he was serving at Winchester College. It was one of three he wrote to be sung by the students at morning, evening, and midnight. Each of Ken's hymns ended with the same four-line verse of praise. Although the three hymns Ken wrote might not be remembered by many, his four lines of praise went on to become the most often-sung hymn in church history. Even today, over three hundred years later, it is sung every Sunday in thousands of Protestant churches. We simply call it "Doxology."

Doxology

Thomas Ken   Traditional

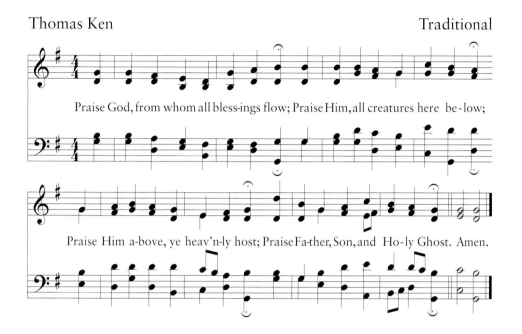

Praise God, from whom all bless-ings flow; Praise Him, all creatures here be-low;

Praise Him a-bove, ye heav'n-ly host; Praise Fa-ther, Son, and Ho-ly Ghost. Amen.

Praise ye the Lord. Praise ye the Lord
from the heavens: praise him in the heights.
Praise ye him, all his angels: praise ye him,
all his hosts. Praise ye him, sun and moon:
praise him, all ye stars of light. Praise him,
ye heavens of heavens, and ye waters that be above
the heavens. Let them praise the name of the Lord:
for he commanded, and they were created...
Let them praise the name of the Lord:
for his name alone is excellent; his glory
is above the earth and heaven. *Psalm 148:1-5, 13*

Joyful, Joyful, We Adore Thee
Henry van Dyke, 1852–1933

A PROFESSOR'S ODE TO JOY

Hymn writers come from all walks of life. Some are highly educated, some without formal schooling, some hold positions in the church, whereas others are businessmen. Henry van Dyke was one who held a variety of positions during his life. He was an ordained minister, a college professor, a successful author and poet, a diplomat, and a chaplain in the United States Navy. Despite his achievements in a variety of fields, his magnificent hymn "Joyful, Joyful, We Adore Thee" remains one of his most enduring legacies.

Henry van Dyke was born in Germantown, Pennsylvania, on November 10, 1852. After graduating from Princeton University, van Dyke took a position as a Congregational pastor in Newport, Rhode Island, where he served for four years before being called to the famous Brick Presbyterian Church in New York City. There, during the next seventeen years, van Dyke distinguished himself as one of America's most outstanding preachers and was selected to serve as a member of the Board of Preachers at Harvard. In addition to his position at Harvard, he frequently visited other universities as a guest lecturer in both English literature and religion.

It was while he was on one of these visits in 1907 that Henry van Dyke wrote the words to his most famous hymn. As a guest of the college president, he was delivering a series of lectures at Williams College in Williamstown, Massachusetts. His upstairs bedroom had a sweeping view of the Berkshire Mountains; and one morning, meditating upon the splendor of the scenery, van Dyke was drawn to compose a poem. He reportedly came down to breakfast that morning, laid the words of his hymn before his host, and stated: "Here is a hymn for you. Your mountains were my inspiration." He later added that he had written the words to be sung to Beethoven's "Hymn of Joy" from the final movement of the composer's ninth symphony. The lyrics combined with the immortal music of Ludwig van Beethoven to create one of the most joyous affirmations of faith in the English language.

Besides his hymns and poems, sermons and college lectures, van Dyke also gained national recognition as an author of books and stories. One of his best-loved pieces is the touching and inspirational Christmas story, *The Other Wiseman*. With all his literary and academic accomplishments, it would seem that Henry van Dyke would have had little time for other pursuits. However, in 1913, he accepted the appointment by President Woodrow Wilson to serve as the United States Minister to the Netherlands and Luxembourg. For four years he filled this position with distinction. When the U. S. became involved in World War I, however, van Dyke resigned his post and accepted a commission as a chaplain in the navy.

When the war ended, van Dyke returned to his preaching, writing, and professorial responsibilities at Princeton University until his retirement in 1923. But even in retirement, he kept busy with a variety of pursuits. He was serving on a committee to revise the Presbyterian *Book of Common Worship* when he passed away on April 10, 1933, at the age of eighty.

Although the life of Henry van Dyke was one of great activity, it was from a few moments of quiet reflection upon the glory of God's creation that he produced his best-loved hymn. Students of hymnology and professors of English have praised van Dyke's hymn poetry as lyrical and sublime, filled with classic images in the best traditions of English literature. But van Dyke held a far different view. When asked to comment upon his work he replied, "These verses are simple expressions of common Christian feelings and desires in this present time—hymns of today that may be sung together by people who know the thought of the age, and are not afraid that any truth of science will destroy religion, or any revolution on earth overthrow the kingdom of heaven. Therefore these are hymns of trust and joy and hope."

Praise the Lord with harp: sing unto him with the psaltery and an instrument of ten strings. Sing unto him a new song; play skillfully with a loud noise. For the word of the Lord is right; and all his works are done in truth. Psalm 33:2–4

Joyful, Joyful, We Adore Thee

Henry van Dyke

Ludwig van Beethoven

1. Joy - ful, joy - ful, we a - dore Thee, God of glo - ry, Lord of love;
2. All Thy works with joy sur-round Thee, Earth and heav'n re-flect Thy rays,
3. Thou art giv - ing and for - giv - ing, Ev - er bless-ing, ev - er blest,
4. Mor-tals, join the might-y cho - rus Which the morn-ing stars be-gan;

Hearts un - fold like flow'rs be-fore Thee, Open-ing to the sun a-bove.
Stars and an - gels sing a-round Thee, Cen - ter of un - bro-ken praise.
Well-spring of the joy of liv - ing, O - cean depth of hap-py rest!
Fa - ther love is reign-ing o'er us, Broth - er love binds man to man.

Melt the clouds of sin and sad-ness, Drive the dark of doubt a-way;
Field and for - est, vale and moun-tain, Flow-ery mead-ow, flash-ing sea,
Thou our Fa - ther, Christ, our Broth-er— All who live in love are Thine;
Ev - er sing-ing, march we on-ward, Vic - tors in the midst of strife,

Giv - er of im - mor-tal glad-ness, Fill us with the light of day.
Chant-ing bird and flow-ing foun-tain, Call us to re - joice in Thee.
Teach us how to love each oth - er, Lift us to the joy di-vine.
Joy - ful mu - sic leads us sun-ward In the tri-umph song of life.

Shall We Gather at the River

Robert Lowry, 1826–1899

A RIVER OF HOPE

Some people just seem to have a natural knack for carpentry or cooking, for decorating or dancing; they do their specialty with great joy and apparent ease. If anyone could be described as having a knack for writing hymns, it would probably be Robert Lowry. Born in Philadelphia on March 12, 1826, Robert had an early interest in music. As a small child he would listen intently to anyone playing an instrument or singing; and from his youngest days, he made up songs to sing to himself. Despite this strong interest in music, Lowry didn't take any classes in either instrumental or vocal music while in school. When he was seventeen, Robert made a commitment to follow God. As a fulfillment of this vow, he attended Bucknell University, graduated with honors, and became a Baptist minister.

Now Lowry's musical interests were turned towards ministry, and he began to think up hymns to use as a part of his preaching and teaching. He still considered his musical abilities no more remarkable than anyone else's natural talents. Asked to describe the process he used in composing his hymns, he replied:

> I watch my moods and when anything strikes me, whether words or
> music, no matter where I am, at home, or on the street, I jot it down.

. . . My brain is a sort of spinning-machine, I think, for there is music running through it all the time. I do not pick out my music on the keys of an instrument. The tunes of nearly all the hymns I have written have been completed on paper before I tried them on the organ. Frequently the words of the hymn and the music have been written at the same time.

Robert Lowry may not have considered his talents extraordinary, but the gospel songs and hymns he shared with his congregation at the Brooklyn Baptist Church began to reach larger and larger audiences. The country was undergoing an explosion in the field of gospel music, and publishing companies were anxious to print collections of songs for church and Sunday school use.

When Lowry was forty years old, a music publisher encouraged him to create a hymnbook for Sunday schools. In the late sixties he began editing materials. In some cases he used poems written by others and composed tunes to accompany them. Two such hymns were "I Need Thee Every Hour" and "Marching to Zion." Many more of the hymns, such as "Nothing But the Blood" and "Up from the Grave He Arose," were solely composed by Lowry. Eventually he published a series of hymnbooks, one volume of which sold over a million copies.

Lowry used the everyday occurrences of his life as inspiration for his hymns, and this was the case with one of his most beloved gospel songs composed in the summer of 1864. New York was sweltering under an oppressive heat wave, and an epidemic raged through the city. Lowry visited with the sick and dying and comforted those who had lost loved ones. One day, he pondered the images of a "river of death" often described in literature. Then, he recalled a Scripture passage from Revelation 22:1 that describes "a pure river of water of life, clear as crystal, proceeding out of the throne of God and of the Lamb." As he continued to meet with grieving families, Lowry comforted them with the verse and the assurance that one day they would reunite with their loved ones beside God's "river of life."

One day, after returning from his rounds exhausted and discouraged, Lowry sat down at his organ and began to idly play the keys. He recalled those in his parish who had lost wives or husbands, brothers and sisters, sons and daughters. Lowry later recorded what happened: "As I mused, the words began to construct themselves. They came first as a question of a Christian inquiry, 'Shall we gather?' Then they broke out in a chorus, as an answer of Christian faith, 'Yes, we'll gather.' On this question and answer the hymn developed itself."

Robert Lowry lived another thirty-five years and composed dozens of hymns until his death in 1899. He is remembered by the gospel music world as a gifted and prolific writer, but Christian congregations around the world remember him for a different reason. They recall him as a fellow pilgrim who reminded them about a river of hope that awaits all God's children.

Shall We Gather at the River

Robert Lowry

Robert Lowry

1. Shall we gath-er at the riv-er, Where bright an-gel feet have trod,
2. On the mar-gin of the riv-er, Wash-ing up its sil-ver spray,
3. Ere we reach the shin-ing riv-er, Lay we ev-'ry bur-den down;
4. Soon we'll reach the shin-ing riv-er, Soon our pil-grim-age will cease;

With its crys-tal tide for - ev - er Flow-ing by the throne of God?
We will walk and wor-ship ev - er, All the hap-py gold - en day.
Grace our spir-its will de - liv - er, And pro-vide a robe and crown.
Soon our hap-py hearts will quiv-er With the mel-o - dy of peace.

Yes, we'll gath-er at the riv-er, the beau - ti-ful, the beau-ti-ful riv-er,

Gath-er with the saints at the riv-er that flows by the throne of God.

Great Is Thy Faithfulness
Thomas O. Chisholm, 1866—?

TRUSTING ONE DAY AT A TIME

Sometimes great hymns are born out of times of struggle or grief, but this triumphant song of faith came from the writer's lifelong experiences of seeing God's faithfulness day by day. It is an affirmation of the unchanging nature of a heavenly Father who not only understands but also delights in meeting His children's needs.

Thomas O. Chisholm knew about God's provision from first-hand experience. Born in a log cabin in Franklin, Kentucky, Chisholm grew up working on the family farm. His formal education ended before high school, but his intellect was keen; and at the age of sixteen, he was hired to teach at the country school he had attended. Only a few years older than many of his students, Thomas must have had daily challenges to his authority as well as his academic abilities. While continuing his teaching responsibilities, he honed his interest in writing by composing poetry and contributing occasional articles to the local weekly newspaper, *The Franklin Favorite*. In 1887, at the age of twenty-one, Chisholm took over as the associate editor of the newspaper. He seemed headed for a successful career in journalism; but when he was twenty-seven, he attended a meeting that would change the course of his life.

In the early 1890s, Dr. H.C. Morrison, a famous American preacher and founder of Asbury College and Theological Seminary, was traveling around the country holding revival meetings. When the evangelist visited Franklin for a series of meetings, Thomas Chisholm decided to attend. It was during one of Dr. Morrison's sermons that Chisholm felt the call of God and decided to dedicate his life to Christian service. After communicating with Chisholm, the preacher offered him the opportunity to move to Louisville in order to serve as business manager and editor of the *Pentecostal Herald*. Trusting in God's provision, Chisholm took the job. After two years of serving in this position, Thomas Chisholm took another step of faith and attended Asbury in order to prepare for the ministry. After receiving his ordination from the Methodist church in 1903, Chisholm was assigned as pastor of a church in Scottsville, Kentucky. His pastoral career was cut short, however, by poor health. He and his family decided to move to Indiana and later to Vineland, New Jersey, where Thomas was able to pursue a less demanding career as an insurance salesman. Despite the disappointment of having to give up the ministry, Chisholm determined to continue in his service to God. He returned to his passion for the written word. Combining that with his call to serve God, and encouraged by Fanny Crosby, one of the most prolific hymn writers to ever live, Chisholm began to produce religious poetry and submit it for publication. By the time of his death, he had published more than eight hundred poems in such periodicals as the *Sunday School Times*, *Moody Monthly*, and *Alliance Weekly*.

Throughout his life, Thomas Chisholm faced disappointment, discouragement, illness, and financial insecurity, but he wrote to a friend: "I must not fail to record here the unfailing faithfulness of a covenant-keeping God and that He has given me many wonderful displays of His providing care, for which I am filled with astonishing gratefulness." It was this unwavering faith in the faithfulness of God that inspired Chisholm to take the words of the prophet Jeremiah from Lamentations 3:22–23, ". . . his compassions fail not. They are new every morning: great is thy faithfulness," and make them the theme of his most famous hymn. The words were not mere theory or philosophy. The writer had seen God fulfill his needs day by day throughout his life. He once said of his writing: "I have sought to be true to the Word, and avoid flippant and catchy titles and treatment. I have greatly desired that each hymn or poem might have some definite message to the hearts for whom it was written." In the writing of "Great Is Thy Faithfulness," the author's desires were surely fulfilled. Millions of hearts have been comforted and assured as Chisholm's hymn has been adopted as a favorite by the Moody Bible Institute, the Billy Graham Crusade, and the students of Bible Study Fellowship International. For those who sing it, the verses echo a personal affirmation of God's continuing pardon, peace, and presence.

Great Is Thy Faithfulness

Thomas O. Chisholm   William M. Runyan

1. Great is Thy faith-ful-ness, O God, my Fa-ther, There is no
2. Sum - mer and win - ter, and spring-time and har-vest, Sun, moon and
3. Par - don for sin and a peace that en - dur-eth, Thine own dear

shad-ow of turn-ing with Thee; Thou chang-est not, Thy com-
stars in their cours-es a - bove Join with all na - ture in
pres-ence to cheer and to guide; Strength for to - day and bright

pas-sions they fail not; As Thou hast been Thou for - ev - er wilt be.
man - i - fold wit-ness To Thy great faith-ful-ness, mer-cy and love.
hope for to - mor-row, Bless-ings all mine, with ten thou-sand be - side!

Great is Thy faith - ful - ness! Great is Thy faith - ful - ness!

Morn-ing by morn-ing new mer-cies I see; All I have need-ed Thy

89

Great Is
Thy
Faithfulness

hand hath pro - vid - ed; Great is Thy faith-ful-ness, Lord, un-to me!

O Love That Will Not Let Me Go
George Matheson, 1842–1906

A SONG IN THE NIGHT

When forty-year-old George Matheson penned the words of his famous hymn on the evening of June 6, 1882, it was under very unusual circumstances. He was staying alone at his home, Innellan Manse, in Innellan on the Clyde in Scotland. The rest of the family was staying overnight in Glasgow in order to celebrate the wedding of George's sister. Matheson, blind from the age of eighteen, reportedly was suffering from a deep distress. The cause of this mental suffering has been a matter of speculation. Many biographers believe it was the memory, prompted by his sister's marriage, of his rejection by a fiancée twenty years earlier. Others feel it was brought on by a more recent loss. Whatever the cause, Matheson reported later that the composition of the hymn was unlike anything else he had ever written:

> It was composed with extreme rapidity; it seemed to me that its construction occupied only a few minutes, and I felt myself rather in the position of one who was being dictated to than an original artist. I was suffering from extreme mental distress, and the hymn was the fruit of pain.

The author also stated that, although he had spent a great deal of his life writing poetry and academic articles, never had he composed a piece that needed no "retouching or correction." The words came, he continued, "like a dayspring from on high." And although he lived another twenty-four years, Matheson said he was "never able to gain once more the same fervor in verse." It was the crowning moment in a life filled with accomplishments as well as pain.

George Matheson was born into a loving Glasgow family on March 27, 1842. Although George was blessed with a brilliant mind, it was apparent from a young age that his eyesight was failing. His wealthy father provided the best education possible for his scholarly son, and the boy entered Glasgow University at the age of fifteen. But there was no remedy for the boy's vision, and by the time he completed his college degree with honors at the age of eighteen, George Matheson was completely blind. Despite their sorrow over their son's loss of sight, the family continued to encourage George to pursue his dreams of becoming a minister. His sister learned Greek, Latin, and Hebrew to help her brother with his theological studies; and when he received his first pastorate, she accompanied him in order to assist with his duties.

Gifted with a brilliant intellect and supported by the love of God and his family, George Matheson began an illustrious career as a Scottish church leader. As a pastor, he served churches in both Edinburgh and Innellan for more than thirty years. At one time, Queen Victoria invited him to preach for her and was so impressed with his sermons that she presented him with a small sculpture of herself as a memento of the occasion. Matheson also distinguished himself in the literary world with his production of many books on theology, logic, and church history, as well as a volume of his original poetry.

But it is the beautiful hymn composed in the night of blindness and despair that has been Matheson's most enduring legacy. In it the images of love, light, joy, and cross beautifully trace the pilgrimage of all who seek to serve the Savior. There is a love that refuses to let us go, yet brings us rest. In the true Light, our spiritual blindness disappears and we see the brightness of God's fairer day. Thus enlightened, we can know a joy that penetrates our pain and suffering. And at the end of life we recognize that it is only through the cross of sacrifice that we find real freedom.

When George Matheson died suddenly at the age of sixty-four, those who loved and lived with him surely found solace in the words he had written two decades earlier: "I trace the rainbow thro' the rain, and feel the promise is not vain that morn shall tearless be."

O Love That Will Not Let Me Go

George Matheson   Albert L. Peace

1. O Love that will not let me go, I rest my wea-ry
2. O Light that fol-low'st all my way, I yield my flick-'ring
3. O Joy that seek-est me thro' pain, I can-not close my
4. O cross that lift-est up my head, I dare not ask to

soul in Thee. I give Thee back the life I owe, That
torch to Thee. My heart re-stores its bor-rowed ray, That
heart to Thee. I trace the rain-bow thro' the rain, And
fly from Thee. I lay in dust life's glo-ry dead, And

in Thine o-cean depths its flow May rich-er, full-er be.
in Thy sun-shine's blaze its day May bright-er, fair-er be.
feel the prom-ise is not vain That morn shall tear-less be.
from the ground there blos-soms red Life that shall end-less be.

*The Lord hath appeared of old unto me,
saying, Yea, I have loved thee
with an everlasting love: therefore with
lovingkindness have I drawn thee.   Jeremiah 31:3*

O Perfect Love
Dorothy Frances Gurney, 1858–1932

A WEDDING GIFT

It is often said that the best gift one can give is something that truly reflects one's heart. If that is true then this beautiful hymn, written by an English poet for her older sister's wedding, was certainly the perfect gift.

Born on October 4, 1858, Dorothy Frances Gurney grew up in a family that valued education and refinement as much as piety and prayer. Dorothy's grandfather had been revered as an Anglican bishop in London, and her father, the Reverend Frederick G. Bloomfield, was the rector of a London parish. Growing up with her sisters in the church parsonage, Dorothy indulged herself with the wealth of literature available in her father's library. At an early age, she demonstrated a remarkable talent for writing verses, and as a young woman she published two volumes of poetry, as well as a book of devotional verses entitled *A Little Book of Quiet*. One of the verses from this work has become a favorite of gardeners throughout the world:

> The kiss of the sun for pardon,
> The song of the birds for mirth:
> One is nearer God's heart in a garden
> Than anywhere else on earth.

The only hymn Dorothy Gurney ever wrote wasn't intended for publication. In fact, it was composed practically on a dare in only fifteen minutes.

The year was 1883 and Dorothy was visiting her soon-to-be-married older sister in the English lake region of Windermere. On one Sunday evening, family and friends were enjoying a time of hymn singing around the piano. They had just finished singing a song entitled "O Strength and Stay." One of the party remarked that it was a shame that such a beautiful melody did not have words suitable for a wedding song. Dorothy's sister agreed and lamented that she was having a terrible time finding a hymn for her upcoming wedding ceremony. At that point, an idea apparently struck the bride-to-be and she turned to her sister.

"What's the use of having a sister who composes poetry if she cannot write new words to a favorite tune? I would like to use this tune at my wedding!" she exclaimed.

Rising to the challenge, Dorothy grabbed the hymnbook, turned to the assembled guests, and replied, "If no one will disturb me, I'll go into the library and see what I can do."

To the astonishment of everyone present, the bride's sister returned in fifteen minutes with a sheet of paper upon which were written the words to "O Perfect Love." The musician played the familiar hymn tune and the guests sang the words Dorothy had written. Immediately her sister declared that she had found the perfect hymn for her wedding! The author later reported, "The writing of [the words] was no effort after the initial idea came to me. I feel God helped me to write this song."

After "O Perfect Love" was first sung at Miss Bloomfield's wedding, it became a great favorite of the social set in London and was sung at several fashionable weddings. In 1898, King George V commissioned Sir Joseph Barnby, a famous English musician, composer, and editor of hymnals, to write a hymn for the marriage of Princess Louise of Wales and the Duke of Fife. Barnby wrote a new melody for "O Perfect Love" and entitled it "Sandringham," after the royal family's residence in Norfolk.

Not long after that, the hymn gained great popularity and was published in several well-known hymnals. We do not know if Dorothy Bloomfield had the song sung at her own wedding when she married Gerald Gurney, but we know that the wedding gift she gave her sister has blessed brides in England and the United States for over a century. When Dorothy Gurney died in 1932 at the age of seventy-four, *The London Times* printed a feature story about her. Despite her fame as a poet, the story began by referring to the only hymn she ever wrote: "Thousands of people at thousands of weddings must have sung, or heard sung, 'O Perfect Love' without ever knowing that Mrs. Gurney was the writer." As with most gifts from the heart, hers had been a far greater blessing than she could ever have imagined.

O Perfect Love

Dorothy F. Gurney   Joseph Barnby

1. O per - fect Love, all hu - man thought tran - scend - ing,
2. O per - fect Life, be Thou their full as - sur - ance
3. Grant them the joy which bright - ens earth - ly sor - row;

Low - ly we kneel in prayer be - fore Thy throne,
Of ten - der char - i - ty and stead - fast faith,
Grant them the peace which calms all earth - ly strife,

That theirs may be the love which knows no end - ing,
Of pa - tient hope and qui - et, brave en - dur - ance,
And to life's day the glo - rious, un - known mor - row

Whom Thou for - ev - er - more dost join in one.
With child - like trust that fears not pain nor death.
That dawns up - on e - ter - nal love and life.

Break Thou the Bread of Life
Mary Lathbury, 1841–1913

Poet Laureate of Chautauqua

During the late nineteenth and early twentieth centuries, an important religious and cultural event took place in the United States. Called the Chautauqua Movement, after the lake where the headquarters and conference grounds stood, it brought educational and cultural opportunities to the American people. Gifted speakers, teachers, musicians, and vocalists traveled throughout the country, giving lectures and bringing performing artists to cities and towns far from the cultural centers of the day. In addition, thousands of people traveled to Lake Chautauqua near Jamestown, New York, to attend conferences held there. They received instruction and training in a variety of fields, including religion.

One of the most active women in the religious education programs offered at Lake Chautauqua was Mary Artemisia Lathbury, who was born in Manchester, New York, on August 10, 1841. Mary's father was the pastor of the Methodist church in Manchester. Her two brothers followed in their father's footsteps and became ministers of the gospel, whereas Mary and her sister pursued their artistic talents. From the time she was very young, Mary demonstrated a remarkable gift for drawing. As she grew older, she developed a talent for writing poetry as well, and by the time of her graduation from school, Mary was sharing an art studio with her older sister in New York. She filled her days teaching art classes, illustrating magazines, and publishing her own collections of poetry illustrated with her original sketches. She was making quite a name for herself in New York, but Mary had a deep desire to do something quite different.

Early in her life, perhaps inspired by her father, Mary developed a longing to be of service to God. Then one day, as she recollected to friends, she seemed to receive clear direction from her Lord: "Remember, my child, that you have a gift of weaving fancies into verse and a gift with the pencil of producing visions that come to your heart; consecrate these to Me as thoroughly as you do your inmost spirit."

Uncertain about how to follow this direction, Mary prayed for guidance and kept on with her writing and illustrating until, in 1874, she was approached by Dr. John H. Vincent, the secretary of the Methodist Sunday School Union. He asked if she would be willing to assist him in planning a summer school specifically for the training of Sunday school teachers. The site for his school was to be in a wooded area along the shore of Lake Chautauqua. Mary saw this as an answer to her prayer for guidance and accepted the offer.

Dr. Vincent's vision would grow into the huge Chautauqua Movement, and Mary's contributions would be manifold. She served Dr. Vincent as a gifted and well-organized secretary. She wrote and edited Methodist Sunday school materials and supervised much of the day-to-day routines at the conference headquarters. Perhaps her greatest contribution, however, was her ability to write hymn texts to complement the themes of Dr. Vincent's sermons. On many occasions, he would request a special hymn; and Mary Lathbury would go off by herself to meditate while overlooking the lake. As she pondered the beauty of the setting, inspiration often came to her, and she would return in a few hours with the completed text for Dr. Vincent.

Her hymn "Break Thou the Bread of Life" was written under just such circumstances. As she sat and watched the rippling blue lake waters, she thought about Jesus miraculously feeding the five thousand beside the Sea of Galilee. In the hymn she begins with the idea of the physical bread broken to feed the hungry crowds and moves to the spiritual image of Christ feeding His followers by breaking open "the Word of truth" so that it may nourish hungry spirits. Her beautiful poetry has been sung during the sacrament of Holy Communion for more than one hundred years and continues to bless congregations today.

Mary composed many other hymns and also began a club for children. Her motto for her young charges was "Look up and not down; look forward and not back; look out and not in; and lend a hand in Jesus' name." Mary Lathbury was a living example of this creed in all she did. At the time of her death in 1913, Mary Lathbury was fondly remembered as a dear friend, a devoted Christian, and the "Poet Laureate and Saint of Chautauqua."

101

Break
Thou
the
Bread
of Life

Break Thou the Bread of Life

Mary A. Lathbury

William F. Sherwin

1. Break Thou the bread of life, Dear Lord, to me,
2. Break Thou the bread of life, O Lord, to me,
3. O - pen Thy Word of Truth That I may see
4. Bless Thou the truth, dear Lord, To me, to me,
5. O send Thy Spir - it, Lord, Now un - to me,

As Thou didst break the loaves Be - side the sea;
That hid with - in my heart Thy Word may be;
Thy mes - sage writ - ten clear And plain for me;
As Thou didst bless the bread By Gal - i - lee;
That He may touch my eyes And make me see;

Be - yond the sa - cred page I seek Thee, Lord;
Mold Thou each in - ward thought, From self set free,
Then in sweet fel - low - ship, Walk - ing with Thee,
Then shall all bond - age cease, All fet - ters fall,
Show me the truth con - cealed With - in Thy Word,

My spir - it pants for Thee, O Liv - ing Word.
And let my steps be all Con - trolled by Thee.
Thine im - age on my life En - graved will be.
And I shall find my peace, My All in All.
And in Thy Book re - vealed I see the Lord.

103

Break
Thou
the
Bread
of Life

To God Be the Glory
Fanny Crosby, 1820-1915

A GRANDMOTHER'S VISION

The six-week-old baby girl lay in her crib, fretful with fever. She would not be comforted by rocking or soothed with nursing. Worried that their daughter's illness was more than just a passing childhood disease, Fanny Crosby's parents called the doctor. After his examination, the physician prescribed poultices be placed upon the infant's eyes and assured the family that their little girl would certainly be better in just a few days. The prognosis was only partly accurate. The baby recovered from her illness, but the doctor's treatment left her permanently blind. It was a tragic mistake that Fanny would carry with her for the next ninety-five years.

Before the family could recover from the shock of their daughter's injuries, they faced another crisis. Fanny's father died suddenly and her mother, left with few financial resources, hired herself out to a wealthy family as a domestic. It was at this point that Fanny's grandmother stepped in and took responsibility for her one-year-old granddaughter's education. She had little money, but she possessed abundant love and a dynamic faith, and these she lavished on the little girl. With determination she stated to a friend, "I will be her eyes."

From that day on, Fanny and her grandmother were constant companions. Each day they took walks as the older woman described in vivid detail sunsets, clouds, trees, flowers, and birds. Her word pictures became Fanny's window to the world. In addition, she opened her granddaughter's eyes of faith. She taught Fanny the stories and poetry of the Bible, and the child demonstrated unusual concentration and an amazing ability for recollection. By the time she was a teenager, Fanny had memorized the first four books of the Bible, all four gospels, the book of Proverbs, many Psalms and several individual chapters of the epistles. In addition to their time spent in study, the older woman and young girl could often be found kneeling side by side in prayer, communing with their Lord and Savior.

When Fanny was fifteen, she left home to enroll at the New York Institution for the Blind. By that time, her loving grandmother had laid the foundation of Christian theology, prayer, memorization, and creative vision that would guide Fanny Crosby for the rest of her life.

She now used her own words to open the eyes of others to the abundant love and compassion of God. She expressed her creative spirit in a variety of ways, but it was through her poetry that Fanny would have the largest impact upon the world. She once said that words and images tumbled into her mind already possessing rhythm and rhyme. It was as if she were empowered by the Spirit of God, for during her lifetime she composed over 8,000 gospel hymns. Often her poems would come to her in the middle of the night and she would lie in the quiet of her room, memorizing the stanzas of dozens of different verses as they played through her mind. In the morning, she would dictate her compositions to her secretary and they would subsequently be published, set to music by a variety of composers, and printed in numerous hymn and songbooks.

While many of Fanny Crosby's admirers viewed her blindness as a great handicap and questioned the Lord's wisdom in allowing the mishap that caused it, Fanny never perceived it that way. Once a well-intentioned Scottish pastor remarked, "I think it is a great pity that the Master, when He showered so many gifts upon you, did not give you sight."

Fanny answered him with a bold rebuke. "Do you know that if at birth I had been able to make one petition to my Creator, it would have been that I should be born blind?"

The startled minister looked shocked as Fanny continued with wonder and joy, "Because when I get to heaven, the first face that shall ever gladden my sight will be that of my Savior!"

Fanny's confidence and optimism no doubt found their roots in the loving acceptance and profound faith of her devoted grandmother. Her hymns ring with a joy based upon sound biblical principles; principles learned in the hours she spent memorizing and discussing Scripture and on her knees in prayer. The resounding theme of her life found no greater expression than in her beautiful hymn "To God Be the Glory." For Fanny Crosby this was far more than the title of a song; it was her credo.

To God Be the Glory

Fanny J. Crosby

William H. Doane

1. To God be the glory, great things He hath done;
2. O perfect redemption, the purchase of blood,
3. Great things He hath taught us, great things He hath done,

So loved He the world that He gave us His Son,
To ev'ry believer the promise of God;
And great our rejoicing through Jesus the Son;

Who yielded His life an atonement for sin,
The vilest offender who truly believes,
But purer and higher, and greater will be

And opened the life-gate that all may go in.
That moment from Jesus a pardon receives.
Our wonder, our transport, when Jesus we see.

Praise the Lord, praise the Lord, Let the earth hear His voice! Praise the

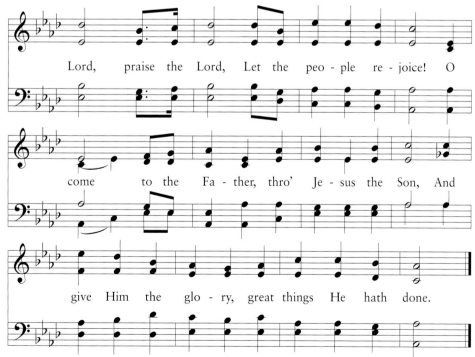

Lord, praise the Lord, Let the peo - ple re - joice! O

come to the Fa - ther, thro' Je - sus the Son, And

give Him the glo - ry, great things He hath done.

My Country, 'Tis of Thee

Samuel Francis Smith, 1808–1895

PENNED BY A PATRIOT

Many great hymn writers are known for the verses they write out of the myriad experiences of a life of faith. This American favorite, often called the country's unofficial national anthem, was the first hymn this twenty-four-year-old seminary student wrote.

During the winter of 1832, Samuel Francis Smith was in his room at the Andover Theological Seminary. Three years earlier, the young man had finished his undergraduate degree at Harvard and now was only six months away from completing his theological studies. The celebrated composer Lowell Mason had given Smith a stack of European music books with the suggestion that the young man, who spoke several languages, might find some hymn worthy of translation and inclusion in a new hymnal Mason was compiling. Smith recounts the events of that day as follows:

One dismal day in February 1832, about half an hour before sunset, I was turning over the leaves of one of the music books when my eye rested on the tune which is now known as "America." I liked the spirited movement of it, not knowing it at that time to be "God Save the King." I glanced at the German words and saw that they were patriotic, and instantly felt the impulse to write a patriotic hymn of my own, adapted to the tune. Picking up a scrap of waste paper which lay near me, I wrote at once, probably within half an hour, the hymn "America" as it is now known everywhere. The whole hymn stands today as it stood on the bit of waste paper, five or six inches long and two-and-a-half wide.

Mason was delighted with the verses, and at the next Independence Day celebration in Boston, he led his children's choir from the Park Street Congregational Church in the first public performance of Smith's anthem.

Young Samuel Smith graduated from Andover Seminary and received his ordination in the Baptist denomination. He went on to pastor many large congregations throughout New England. In addition to his pastoral duties, he continued with his linguistic studies and eventually learned to speak and read fifteen languages. Recognizing the power of hymns to inspire worship, he wrote more than 150 of them during his lifetime. Throughout his life, however, Smith's passion was for missions. Although he never served overseas in this capacity, he did, in 1860, resign from his church in Waterville, Maine, to become the secretary of the Baptist Missionary Union. In this position he traveled overseas and visited missionaries serving in Europe and Asia. During these journeys he wrote of the joy of hearing his missionary hymn "The Morning Light Is Breaking" sung wherever he went. He reported, "It has been a great favorite at missionary gatherings, and I have myself heard it sung in five or six different languages in Europe and Asia."

Samuel Francis Smith's accomplishments, both in the pulpit and behind university lecterns as a professor of linguistics, gained him a reputation as a distinguished writer and teacher; but his fame in the United States is eclipsed by his first hymn, the patriotic verses known as "America" or "My Country 'Tis of Thee."

It is said that on one of his trips around the country, Smith stopped in Chicago to visit the Board of Trade. As he observed the activity of the financial brokers on the floor below, word spread that the writer of "America" was seated in the viewers' gallery. One by one, as the traders became aware of his presence, they stopped their activity and gazed up to see the famous man. Then, spontaneously, the assembly began to sing "My Country 'Tis of Thee." Moved by their tribute, Smith asked to be escorted to the floor, where he joined the impromptu choir in singing the remaining verses.

Until the end of his life, Samuel Francis Smith worked tirelessly to increase the capacity of his mind and spirit. At the age of eighty-seven he decided to take up the study of Russian, and when he passed away one year later on November 19, 1895, he was on a train traveling to a preaching engagement near Boston. His was a life filled with accomplishment and purpose; and like the anthem he wrote for his beloved nation, his influence for God and country continues to be remembered more than a century after his death.

My Country, 'Tis of Thee

Samuel F. Smith

Traditional

1. My coun-try, 'tis of thee, Sweet land of lib-er-ty, Of thee I sing: Land where my fa-thers died, Land of the pil-grims' pride, From ev-'ry moun-tain-side Let free-dom ring.
2. My na-tive coun-try, thee, Land of the no-ble free, Thy name I love: I love thy rocks and rills, Thy woods and tem-pled hills; My heart with rap-ture thrills Like that a-bove.
3. Let mu-sic swell the breeze And ring from all the trees Sweet free-dom's song: Let mor-tal tongues a-wake, Let all that breathe par-take; Let rocks their si-lence break, The sound pro-long.
4. Our fa-thers' God, to Thee, Au-thor of lib-er-ty, To Thee we sing: Long may our land be bright With free-dom's ho-ly light; Pro-tect us by Thy might, Great God, our King!

Blessed is the nation whose God is the Lord; and the people whom he hath chosen for his own inheritance. The Lord looketh from heaven; he beholdeth all the sons of men. From the place of his habitation he looketh upon all the inhabitants of the earth...Let thy mercy, O Lord, be upon us, according as we hope in thee. Psalm 33:12-14, 22

This Is My Father's World
Maltbie D. Babcock, 1858–1901

An Athlete's Praises

Maltbie D. Babcock was born to a socially prominent family in Syracuse, New York, on August 3, 1858. Early in his life, it was clear that he would be no ordinary young man when he demonstrated talents in areas many might consider contradictory. He wrote deeply spiritual poetry, yet had a great love for jokes and mischief. On the playing field he was a fierce competitor and a brilliant athlete, yet he loved music and became skilled at the organ, piano, and violin. He relished the outdoors but willingly spent hours at his studies.

By the time he completed his high school education, many of his teachers and coaches believed he was headed for greatness. While attending Syracuse University, he became an outstanding college athlete and distinguished himself as a baseball pitcher and swimmer. But as powerful as he was physically, Maltbie Babcock's real strength lay in his mind and spirit.

Known for his character and integrity, the young man determined to pursue a career in God's service and became one of the most outstanding Presbyterian ministers of his generation. Putting his talents of writing, music, study, and athletics under the leadership of his Lord, Babcock led his congregations with a challenge to live as active Christians. In one of his poems he defined this conviction as follows:

Be strong!
We are not here to play, to dream, to drift,
We have hard work to do, and loads to lift.
Shun not the struggle; face it. 'Tis God's gift.

Be strong!
Say not the days are evil—who's to blame?
And fold the hands and acquiesce—O shame!
Stand up, speak out, and bravely—in God's Name.

Be strong!
It matters not how deep intrenched the wrong,
How hard the battle goes, the day how long.
Faint not, fight on! Tomorrow comes the song.

Because of his physical strength, strong convictions, and dynamic personality, it is not surprising that the young men of Babcock's congregations respected their pastor. He brought out the best in those he led and was well-known for his keen sense of justice and fair play. At times these were demonstrated in ways one might not suspect a pastor would use. On one occasion, when Babcock witnessed an older fellow bullying a younger boy and taunting him with foul language, the pastor decided to teach the offender a lesson. Quietly approaching from the rear, Babcock silently seized the bully by the nape of the neck and the seat of the pants, gave him a couple of swings, and then launched him over a nearby fence. As he had often told his young parishioners, "actions speak louder than words."

Making exercise a lifelong habit, Pastor Babcock regularly took brisk morning walks. Often as he was leaving his home he would call out, "I'm going out to see my Father's world." To him the world was indeed a reflection of God's glory. Meditating upon this theme, the minister composed a lengthy poem of praise. In its original form, the poem contains sixteen verses, each one amplifying upon the previous to explore the nature of God through the prism of His creation. It begins as a tribute to the physical world and ends with a personal commitment to remain strong, to do right, and to look for the day when the purposes of God and mankind will finally be united.

Although he was a gifted musician and composer, Babcock never had the opportunity to set "This Is My Father's World" to music. In 1901, while returning from a trip to the Holy Land with his wife, the dynamic man suddenly passed away at the age of only forty-three. F. L. Sheppard, an accomplished composer and friend of the Babcocks, adapted an old English melody to fit with the words of the poem; and in 1915 it was published as a hymn in a Presbyterian Sunday school book. Since that time, Maltbie Babcock's hymn of praise has been included in hymnals all over the world, reminding believers everywhere that the earth and all who dwell in it belong to the Heavenly Father.

This Is My Father's World

Maltbie D. Babcock   Franklin L. Sheppard

1. This is my Fa-ther's world, And to my lis-t'ning ears, All
2. This is my Fa-ther's world, The birds their car-ols raise; The
3. This is my Fa-ther's world, O let me ne'er for-get That

na - ture sings, and round me rings The mu - sic of the spheres.
morn - ing light, the lil - y white De - clare their Mak-er's praise.
though the wrong seems oft so strong, God is the Rul - er yet.

This is my Fa-ther's world, I rest me in the thought Of
This is my Fa-ther's world, He shines in all that's fair; In the
This is my Fa-ther's world: The bat - tle is not done; Je -

rocks and trees, of skies and seas; His hand the won - ders wrought.
rust - ling grass I hear Him pass, He speaks to me ev - 'ry - where.
sus who died shall be sat - is - fied, And earth and heav'n be one.

Angels, from the Realms of Glory

James Montgomery, 1771–1854

FROM SUFFERING TO GLORY

From a very young age, James Montgomery understood suffering. Born at Irvine, Ayrshire, Scotland, on November 4, 1771 to Moravian missionaries, it was decided when he was just a small boy that he would follow in the footsteps of his parents. At the age of seven, he was sent to England to study for his vocation at the Moravian seminary in Fulneck, Yorkshire. The little boy had a sensitive spirit and even at that young age began to pour out his feelings in poetry.

After James was at the seminary for five years, his parents were sent to the West Indies. When he bid them farewell, he never imagined it would be the last time he would see them. At the age of twelve, James was orphaned; and because he lacked funds to continue his schooling, he was placed in the care of a couple within the Moravian community. The boy's depression and his pensive nature caused them to label him a dreamer who "never had a sense of the hour." Fearing he would end up unable to support himself, they tried to help him locate an apprenticeship in a local business. For a time, James worked as a clerk's assistant, but the labor bored him and left him little time for his true passion of writing. He then took a position as a baker's assistant. Although the work was tedious, it was not particularly demanding, and James found he could compose verses when business was slow.

By the time James was nineteen, he knew that he was not cut out to be a shopkeeper or a baker. He packed up his collection of poems and headed for London in search of a publisher. Traveling from editor to editor, the hopeful young author was met with the same reception at each stop: not interested. The ordinarily melancholy Montgomery fell into a fresh despair. Alone, discouraged, penniless, and unemployed, he left London and returned to Wath, the place of his last employment. There, after a time of aimlessness, he found a position assisting Robert Gales, editor of the local newspaper, *The Sheffield Register*.

Finally he had a position where his gifts for writing could be appreciated. But Montgomery's employer was involved in radical political causes and published several articles arousing the fury of the local authorities. With little warning, Gales packed up and headed for America, leaving twenty-three-year-old James to take over the paper. Undaunted by his latest reversal of fortune, the new editor decided to make the best of the situation. He renamed the paper *The Sheffield Iris* and began to write editorials and articles himself. Unfortunately, he had as little discretion as his predecessor; and within two years, the local government had twice thrown him into jail. Things were going from bad to worse, but despite bouts of depression, Montgomery determined to continue with his paper.

He would serve as its editor for over thirty years. During that time James Montgomery published his first collection of poetry and entitled it *Prison Amusements*, since several of the pieces had been written during his imprisonment in the Sheffield jail. It was the first in a long line of published works.

In all, James Montgomery published several works of prose and over four hundred poems, more than half of which were set to music and sung as hymns. In addition, he was recognized for his contribution to the literature of England and was awarded a pension equivalent to one thousand dollars a year. Just a few months before his death in 1854, at the age of eighty-three, Montgomery was asked which of his poems he thought would be best remembered by the world. The elderly writer thought for a few moments and then sadly whispered, "None, sir; nothing, except perhaps a few of my hymns."

Montgomery may not have realized how prophetic those words would be. Although he contributed much to the literary world of his time, it is through his hymns that he has reached beyond his generation. Despite the suffering and depression he experienced most of his life, James Montgomery gave the world such magnificent hymns of praise as "Hail to the Lord's Anointed," "O Spirit of the Living God," "Forever with the Lord," and the beautiful Christmas carol "Angels, from the Realms of Glory."

117

Angels,

from

the

Realms

of

Glory

Angels, from the Realms of Glory

James Montgomery   Henry Smart

1. An - gels, from the realms of glo - ry, Wing your flight o'er
2. Shep-herds, in the fields a - bid - ing, Watch-ing o'er your
3. Sa - ges, leave your con - tem-pla - tions, Bright - er vi - sions
4. Saints be - fore the al - tar bend-ing, Watch-ing long in
5. Tho' an in - fant now we view Him, He will share His

all the earth; Ye who sang cre - a - tion's sto - ry,
flocks by night, God with man is now re - sid - ing,
beam a - far; Seek the great De - sire of na - tions,
hope and fear, Sud - den - ly the Lord, de-scend - ing,
Fa - ther's throne; Gath - er all the na - tions to Him;

Now pro - claim Mes - si - ah's birth:
Yon - der shines the in - fant Light.
Ye have seen His na - tal star: Come and wor - ship,
In His tem - ple shall ap - pear:
Ev - 'ry knee shall then bow down:

come and wor - ship, Wor - ship Christ, the new-born King.

119

Angels,

from

the

Realms

of

Glory

I Love Thy Kingdom, Lord
Timothy Dwight, 1752–1817

THE FIRST AMERICAN HYMN

For those of us used to singing hymns and praise songs, it is difficult to understand that these forms of worship were once seen as inappropriate. Prior to the Great Awakening of the eighteenth century, the only form of singing acceptable in the church was the chanting or recitation of Psalms. The verses in the Bible were considered sacred and sufficient for worship.

In the eighteenth century, churches in England were recognizing the power of hymns written to reflect God's power, glory, and grace. Evangelists such as Isaac Watts, John Newton, Charles Wesley, and Augustus Toplady were enriching Christian worship with such hymns as "Love So Amazing, So Divine," "Amazing Grace," "O for a Thousand Tongues to Sing," and "Rock of Ages." But in America, the influence of the Puritans and their *Bay Psalmist* book of Psalms still prevailed in churches across New England. All that was to change, however, because of one man who would become known as the "Father of American Hymnody."

Timothy Dwight was born into a family of Christian accomplishment. From pulpits across New England, Timothy's grandfather Jonathan Edwards led the Great Awakening of the 1730s and 1740s. Shortly after Timothy's birth, his mother began teaching him from the Scriptures; and by the time the boy was four, he was able to read the Bible. Possessing a keen mind and a love for learning, Timothy Dwight entered Yale University at the age of thirteen and was graduated with highest honors shortly after his seventeenth birthday. After his graduation and ordination as a minister, Dwight served as a chaplain for George Washington in the Revolutionary War. During his tour of duty, it was his custom to write songs to encourage the colonial troops. At the conclusion of the war, Dwight returned to his ministry as a Congregationalist preacher, traveling throughout the New England states. In addition to his career as a minister of the gospel, Dwight maintained a farm in Connecticut and served for a time as a representative in the legislature of that state. In 1795, Timothy Dwight was selected as president of his alma mater, Yale University, and returned to that institution with a determination to bring it back to its Christian roots.

When he took the presidency of Yale, it was reported that the prevailing philosophy within the student body was that of the French Revolutionist Rousseau and the American free thinker Thomas Paine. There was a rejection of belief in Christ, the existence of miracles, the inspiration of the Bible, and anything that conflicted with intellectual reason. In fact, it was noted in school records that only one graduate in the class of 1800 was a church member. Timothy Dwight had his work cut out for him.

During the last forty years of his life, Dwight's dynamic preaching, teaching, writing, and leadership ignited a spiritual revival on campus. Yale began sending Christian evangelists to other campuses across the eastern United States and into the mission fields around the world. As a part of this spiritual renewal, Timothy Dwight edited and published a collection of hymns containing several works by English authors, as well as his original verses expressing the truths of the Christian faith. Published in 1800, his hymn "I Love Thy Kingdom, Lord" is widely recognized as the earliest hymn of American origin still in common use today.

Timothy Dwight used his position of leadership and influence at Yale to infuse the Christian church with the power of song. He utilized his intellect to increase the body of theological thought with his volumes of sermons. And he contributed to the history of America through his four historical volumes entitled *Travels in New England and New York*.

These achievements alone should have certainly secured his place in the history of the United States, but what made this man's life even more remarkable was that during the last four decades of his life—when the largest body of his written work was accomplished—Timothy Dwight was afflicted with a severe physical disability. After a bout of smallpox, his eyes were so damaged that he experienced constant and agonizing pain. The brilliant scholar, teacher, and preacher could not read or write for more than fifteen minutes at a time. Despite his handicap, Timothy Dwight refused to yield to self-pity. In keeping with the traditions of his family and faith, he focused steadily not upon his limitations but, as he declares in the final phrase of his most famous hymn, the "brighter bliss of heav'n."

I Love Thy Kingdom, Lord

Timothy Dwight

Aaron Williams

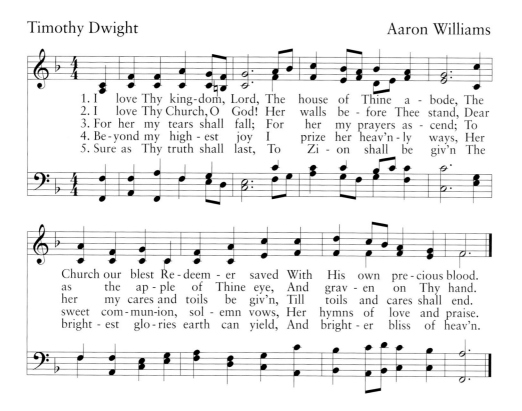

1. I love Thy king-dom, Lord, The house of Thine a - bode, The
2. I love Thy Church, O God! Her walls be - fore Thee stand, Dear
3. For her my tears shall fall; For her my prayers as - cend; To
4. Be-yond my high - est joy I prize her heav'n - ly ways, Her
5. Sure as Thy truth shall last, To Zi - on shall be giv'n The

Church our blest Re - deem - er saved With His own pre - cious blood.
as the ap - ple of Thine eye, And grav - en on Thy hand.
her my cares and toils be giv'n, Till toils and cares shall end.
sweet com - mun-ion, sol - emn vows, Her hymns of love and praise.
bright - est glo - ries earth can yield, And bright - er bliss of heav'n.

All thy works shall praise thee, O Lord;
and thy saints shall bless thee. They shall speak
of the glory of thy kingdom, and talk of thy power;
To make known to the sons of men his mighty acts,
and the glorious majesty of his kingdom. Thy kingdom
is an everlasting kingdom, and thy dominion
endureth throughout all generations.   Psalm 145:10-13

Leaning on the Everlasting Arms

Elisha Hoffman, 1839—1929 and Anthony Showalter, 1858—1924

A COLLABORATION OF CONSOLATION

In America prior to the nineteenth century, the study of music was a subject left to institutions of higher learning and those wealthy enough to afford private lessons. Consequently, few people could read musical scores or sing from the notes on a page. Lowell Mason, a bank clerk who later became a famous American composer, was determined to develop a system of bringing musical education to the masses. He published songbooks and trained music teachers to use them, then sent these trained individuals to a variety of towns in rural America. Before long, music education became a recognized subject in the public schools.

In addition to music classes during school hours, many of these so-called "music masters" conducted lessons after school and during the evenings. One such teacher of the Mason method was Anthony Showalter. Traveling throughout the southern United States, Showalter conducted music schools in various communities for weeks at a time. His classes were well-attended, and men and women of all ages took advantage of his instruction in the reading of vocal music.

In 1887, Showalter was conducting a singing school in Hartselle, Alabama. After bidding farewell to his last students of the day, the teacher packed up his music books, closed up the church building he was using for his lessons, and walked back into town to the boardinghouse where he was staying. He wrote to a friend, relating what happened next:

> I received a letter from two of my former pupils in South Carolina, conveying the sad intelligence that on the same day each of them had buried his wife. . . . I tried to console them by writing a letter that might prove helpful in their hour of sadness. Among other Scriptures I quoted this passage, "The eternal God is your refuge, and underneath are the everlasting arms" (Deuteronomy 33:27). Before completing the writing of the sentence, the thought came to me that the fact that we may lean on these everlasting arms and find comfort and strength ought to be put in a song; and before finishing that letter, the words and music of the refrain were written.

The refrain, however, was all that Showalter could produce. He seemed blocked from composing additional stanzas. Convinced that he had the beginnings of a hymn that would bring comfort to his former students, the music teacher copied the refrain and melody and sent it off to Elisha Hoffman, a composer and writer residing in Pennsylvania. Hoffman had already made a name for himself in the world of hymn-writing, having produced over two thousand compositions. As busy as he was, the composer's interest was sparked by Showalter's touching request, and he immediately focused his attention upon the music teacher's refrain: "Leaning, leaning, safe and secure from all alarms; / Leaning, leaning, leaning on the everlasting arms."

Within a few days, Elisha Hoffman completed three stanzas to accompany the refrain and sent them back to Showalter for his approval. The collaboration had resulted in exactly what the music teacher had hoped. He sent off the completed song to his grieving students, and Hoffman published it in his 1887 *Glad Evangel for Revival, Camp and Evangelistic Meetings Hymnal*. Since that time, the comforting gospel song has been translated into several languages and reprinted in more than five-hundred different gospel songbooks. There is no record of how the young widowers were comforted by this famous song; but for more than one hundred years, it has brought solace to thousands who struggle with trusting God during times of sorrow. When reason and intellect fail to bring satisfaction, there comes a time when we each may need to fall into the embrace of faith by "leaning on the everlasting arms."

*Trust in the Lord with all thine heart;
and lean not unto thine own understanding.
In all thy ways acknowledge him,
and he shall direct thy paths. Proverbs 3:5—6*

Leaning on the Everlasting Arms

Elisha A. Hoffman

Anthony J. Showalter

1. What a fel-low-ship, what a joy di-vine, Lean-ing on the ev-er-
2. Oh, how sweet to walk in this pil-grim way, Lean-ing on the ev-er-
3. What have I to dread, what have I to fear, Lean-ing on the ev-er-

last-ing arms; What a bless-ed-ness, what a peace is mine,
last-ing arms; Oh, how bright the path grows from day to day,
last-ing arms? I have bless-ed peace with my Lord so near,

Lean-ing on the ev-er-last-ing arms. Lean - ing,
Lean-ing on the ev-er-last-ing arms. Lean - ing,
Lean-ing on the ev-er-last-ing arms. Lean-ing on Je-sus,

lean - ing,
lean-ing on Je-sus, safe and se-cure from all a-larms;

lean - ing, lean - ing,
lean-ing on Je-sus, lean-ing on Je-sus, lean-ing on the ev-er-last-ing arms.

The Solid Rock
Edward Mote, 1797—1874

FROM CABINETRY TO CHRIST

During the winter of 1797, the slums of London were cold and dismal. In the damp chill of an upper room in a cheap public house, Edward Mote was born into poverty. Young Edward grew up on the streets and described himself in these words: "So ignorant was I that I did not know that there was a God." The school he attended for a few years neither allowed any teaching from the Scriptures nor permitted a Bible to be seen on the premises. Until his mid-teens the young boy had never been inside a church, heard a sermon, prayed a prayer, or sung a hymn.

Shortly after his sixteenth birthday, however, Edward's life took a dramatic turn. At the age of sixteen, Edward left the streets and the classroom for an apprenticeship with a London cabinetmaker. The man was not only a fine craftsman but also a devout Christian, and he took his young charge to church with him on Sundays. One day, the famous preacher Reverend John Hyatt was speaking at Tottenham Court Road Chapel. The cabinetmaker and his apprentice attended one of Hyatt's services. Something in the preacher's words struck a chord in Edward's heart, causing him to re-evaluate his life. Shortly thereafter, the young man decided to devote his life to following Christ.

Edward returned home with his master and continued to learn the carpentry trade until he was able to move to the suburb of Southwark and establish his own shop. There he worked diligently at his trade and became an active member of a local Baptist congregation. But the devoted carpenter prayed to have a life that counted for God in a special way.

While he waited upon God to answer his prayer, Mote ministered as a layperson to those in his church. At times, the busy carpenter would transfer his thoughts about God into verses, which he would then share when the opportunity arose. It was on one such occasion in 1834 that the words to his most famous hymn, "The Solid Rock," were written.

On the way to work one morning, the words "on Christ the solid rock I stand, all other ground is sinking sand" kept ringing in his mind. He jotted them onto a piece of paper; and later, when time allowed, added four verses to accompany this chorus. For some reason, he folded the paper and stuck it in his pocket the following Sunday morning as he headed off to worship services. Leaving church that day, Mote encountered a Mr. King, who shared that his wife was gravely ill and wondered if Mote would consider visiting the woman later that afternoon. Agreeing, the cabinetmaker arrived at the King residence just as the family began their time of evening devotions. It was their custom to read the Bible, pray, and sing a hymn together, but they could not locate their family hymnbook. At that moment, Mote remembered the verses in his pocket and offered to share them with the family. After singing the poem, the family seemed greatly encouraged, and the sick woman requested a copy so she might read it over again. Happily, Mote returned to his home, composed an additional two verses, and sent the completed text to the King residence.

Edward Mote may have wondered if his prayer to speak for God was being answered through his written rather than his spoken words; but it would become clear that God had even more in mind for the humble cabinetmaker. In 1847, the members of his Baptist congregation decided to take on the challenge of building their own church in Horsham, Sussex. Mote worked tirelessly on the construction efforts; and when the building was completed, the grateful parishioners offered him the deed to the property. The cabinetmaker refused, requesting instead that he be given access to the pulpit for as long as he continued to preach faithfully. His fellow church members gladly granted his request; and at the age of fifty-one, Mote finally realized his dream of becoming a preacher.

For the next twenty-six years, Edward Mote served as the pastor of this Baptist congregation; and when he neared death in 1874, he stated with confidence, "I think I am nearing Port. But the truths I have preached I am living upon, and they will do to die upon!" Indeed, the little boy who had grown up on the slippery paving stones of a London slum had found firm footing on the solid rock of Christ!

The Solid Rock

Edward Mote   William B. Bradbury

1. My hope is built on noth-ing less Than Je-sus' blood and right-eous-ness;
2. When dark-ness veils His love-ly face, I rest on His un-chang-ing grace;
3. His oath, his cov - e - nant, his blood, Sup-port me in the whelm-ing flood;
4. When He shall come with trum-pet sound, Oh, may I then in Him be found;

I dare not trust the sweet-est frame, But whol-ly lean on Je-sus' name.
In ev-'ry high and storm-y gale, My an-chor holds with-in the veil.
When all a-round my soul gives way, He then is all my hope and stay.
Dressed in His right-eous-ness a - lone, Fault-less to stand be - fore the throne.

On Christ, the sol - id Rock, I stand; All oth - er ground

is sink - ing sand, All oth - er ground is sink - ing sand.

Come, Ye Thankful People, Come
Henry Alford, 1810—1871

THE ATTITUDE OF GRATITUDE

This favorite Thanksgiving hymn was written in 1844 by the Dean of Canterbury Cathedral, Henry Alford. The famous English scholar, teacher, preacher, and writer spent his entire life fulfilling a promise made to God when he was only sixteen years old; and in his beautiful hymn of thanks, he relates the source of his motivation–that of gratitude.

Henry Alford was born on a chilly fall day in October of 1810 into a long line of Anglican preachers. Raised and educated in the best schools of his time, exposed to excellent preaching, and trained early in the truths of Scripture, it was not a surprise when the youth wrote the following vow in his Bible: "I do this day, in the presence of God and my own soul, renew my covenant with God, and solemnly determine henceforth to become His and to do His work as far as in me lies."

This spirit of devotion and diligence would be the hallmark of Alford's life. After completing his secondary education, he enrolled at Trinity College, Cambridge, where he made a name for himself as both a student and a writer. Upon graduation, he began a period of public ministry in and around London and rose quickly within the Anglican Church. He was not afraid of controversy and repeatedly engaged in debates opposing those working to move the Anglicans toward a "high church" position. Despite his busy preaching and teaching schedule, he maintained a rigorous routine of writing. His efforts on behalf of literary scholarship were renowned even during his lifetime. He authored numerous books of poetry, literary criticism, and church history; but his finest literary achievement was his four-volume edition of the Greek New Testament on which he labored for twenty years. It was used by biblical scholars as the standard critical commentary during the latter part of the nineteenth century.

It would be logical to assume that a man of so many personal achievements and such wide-spread fame might be arrogant and self-important, but those who knew Henry Alford noted he was neither. Biographers have described him as a "pious young student, an eloquent preacher, a sound biblical critic, a man of great learning and taste, one of the most gifted men of his day, and an affectionate man, full of good humour." He consistently gave credit for his accomplishments to God. And it was commonly known that the Dean of Canterbury stood at the end of each meal and again at the end of the day to offer thanks to God for the many blessings of life. In all things he strove to demonstrate an attitude of gratitude.

Perhaps Henry Alford's one fault was that he refused to rest. Driven by a force within himself, he spent his days moving from one activity to another, ministering to the needs of the cathedral, always working on a new project, never taking the time to relax. In the end, his unrelenting work ethic prevented him from fulfilling one of his greatest dreams—making a trip to the Holy Land. When he died at the age of sixty-one from what his physicians called a "physical breakdown," the inscription on his tombstone was an acknowledgment of this unfulfilled dream. It read: "The Inn of a Pilgrim Traveling to Jerusalem."

One wonders, however, how Alford himself would have viewed the situation. In his hymn "Come, Ye Thankful People, Come" he refers to the time when God gathers in the faithful like a farmer harvesting his fields. He paints a picture of a glorious place where even those whose work on earth is unending will find a place to finally be at rest. Perhaps Henry Alford would have viewed his death as he did his life: another opportunity to give thanks to the Lord of the harvest who finally brought him home.

Know ye that the Lord he is God:
it is he that hath made us, and not we ourselves;
we are his people, and the sheep of his pasture.
Enter into his gates with thanksgiving,
and into his courts with praise: be thankful
unto him and bless his name. Psalm 100:3–4

Come, Ye Thankful People, Come

Henry Alford   George J. Elvey

1. Come, ye thank-ful peo-ple, come; Raise the song of har-vest home.
2. All the world is God's own field, Fruit un - to His praise to yield,
3. For the Lord our God shall come And shall take His har-vest home,
4. E - ven so, Lord, quick - ly come To Your fi - nal har-vest home,

All is safe - ly gath-ered in Ere the win-ter storms be - gin.
Wheat and tares to - geth - er sown, Un - to joy or sor - rows grown.
From His field shall in that day All of-fens-es purge a - way,
Gath - er all Your peo - ple in, Free from sor-row, free from sin,

God, our Mak - er, doth pro - vide For our wants to be sup-plied;
First the blade, and then the ear, Then the full corn shall ap - pear,
Give His an - gels charge at last In the fire the tares to cast,
There, for - ev - er pu - ri - fied, In Your pres-ence to a - bide.

Come to God's own tem - ple, come, Raise the song of har-vest home.
Lord of har - vest, grant that we Whole-some grain and pure may be.
But the fruit-ful ears to store In His gar - ner ev - er-more.
Come, with all Your an - gels, come, Raise the glo - rious har-vest home.

All Things Bright and Beautiful
Cecil Frances Alexander, 1818?–1895

FROM THE HEART OF A CHILD

When Cecil Alexander was just a little girl, she found great delight in writing poetry. Although she loved writing her verses, she was certain her father would find them silly and frivolous because he was an officer in the Royal Marines and known for his stern manner and military bearing. Fearing his disapproval but unwilling to stop her writing, Cecil hid her poems under the carpet in her bedroom.

One evening, when the girl was only nine years old, her father discovered her cache of verses. Expecting a scolding, Cecil was surprised when her father not only praised her efforts but also, the next day, presented her with a box in which to store her compositions. Thereafter, the two of them set aside a time every Saturday evening when Cecil would bring her box of poems to her father and he would read them aloud and offer helpful and encouraging comments.

Thus encouraged, the little Irish girl developed her natural gift for writing. Even as she grew older, she maintained the childlike simplicity of her verses and believed that her calling was to present the truths of Scripture in a manner so clear that even a young child could understand them. As a teenager, she realized that the church catechism and Apostles' Creed were filled with words and concepts that most children (and many adults) did not understand. When her godchildren complained that they found their religion lessons too difficult, she determined to find a way to help them. Cecil took each part of the catechism and wrote verses illustrating the truths of such subjects as the Trinity, baptism, the Ten Commandments, and the Lord's Prayer. By the time she was in her early twenties, she had composed hundreds of poems; and in 1848 she published a volume of poetry entitled *Hymns for Little Children*. The dedication to her book reads:

> To my little Godsons, I inscribe these lines hoping that the language of the verse, which children love, may help to impress on their minds what they are, what I have promised for them, and what they must seek to be.

Included in this volume were several of Cecil Alexander's hymns that remain popular today, including "All Things Bright and Beautiful," "Once in Royal David's City," "Jesus Calls Us O'er the Tumult," and "There Is a Green Hill Far Away."

Two years after completing her first published work, Cecil married William Alexander, the young rector of a local parish church in Tyrone, Ireland. Together they set out to minister to the parishioners in their impoverished rural area. Cecil's love and concern for children now extended to all the needy in the area; and she was often seen going from home to home carrying food and clothing and bringing comfort to the sick and dying. Her husband wrote a tribute to her kindness in the following words: "From one poor home to another, from one bed of sickness to another, from one sorrow to another, she went. Christ was ever with her and in her and all felt her influence."

The Reverend William Alexander rose in the church to become archbishop of all Ireland, but his humble wife never forgot those less fortunate than she. When her book *Hymns for Little Children* reached the status of a bestseller by 1872, having sold 414,000 copies, Cecil Alexander donated the royalties to support handicapped children in northern Ireland. Although her husband was accorded great honors in his position of archbishop, he once remarked that he would be remembered only as the husband of a great hymn-writer. His words proved to be true. Although Cecil Alexander died in 1895, sixteen years before her husband, it is her name that is found in hymnals around the world more than a century after her death.

Cecil Alexander never lost her childlike faith or her ability to connect with the child in each person who sings her hymns. From a shy child who hid her gifts under a carpet, she became a woman of faith who generously shared the wise and wonderful things she learned with the rest of God's family.

139

All
Things
Bright
and
Beautiful

All Things Bright and Beautiful

Cecil F. Alexander   L.O. Sanderson

1. The lit - tle flow'r that o - pens, The lit - tle bird that sings
2. The cold wind in the win - ter, The pleas-ant sum - mer sun,
3. He gave us eyes to see them, And lips that we might tell

God made their glow-ing col - ors, He made their ti - ny wings.
The ripe fruits in the gar - den, He made them ev - 'ry one.
How great is God Al - might - y, Who has made all things well.

All things bright and beau-ti-ful, Crea-tures great and small,

All things wise and won-der-ful, The Lord God made them all.

141

All
Things
Bright
and
Beautiful

His Name Is Wonderful

Audrey Mieir, 1916—

AN UNEXPECTED CHRISTMAS BLESSING

It was December 1959 and the evening of the annual Christmas program at the Bethel Union Church in Duarte, California. The sanctuary had been decorated with fragrant pine boughs, and a replica of the Bethlehem stable was placed in the front of the room. For weeks the young people of the congregation had been learning their parts, memorizing Christmas carols, and practicing the pageant that would be their gift to the congregation this Christmas season.

Finally, the evening of the presentation arrived. Audrey Mieir, an active member of the congregation and sister-in-law of the pastor, sat among those waiting for the program to begin. Softly, the strains of the first hymn began. Joseph, a local high school student dressed in his father's bathrobe, walked slowly down the aisle and tried not to look embarrassed. Mary, one of his classmates, gingerly held his arm and attempted to look serene as she worked to match his long strides. Every now and then, she'd peek shyly from under the pale blue shawl covering her head. When the holy family arrived at the stable, they took their places behind a straw-filled cradle and miraculously brought forth their firstborn, a doll from the nursery department, wrapped him in swaddling clothes, and laid him in the waiting straw as the children's choir sang "Away in a Manger."

Meanwhile, on the hills of Bethlehem located slightly to the rear, the shepherds were busy watching invisible flocks of sheep. They jumped to their feet in fear and trembling as a small band of pillowcase-clad angels approached, then directed them to observe the star that dangled over the baby Jesus. With expressions intended to approximate awe, the shepherds trekked off to find the Savior and soon gathered near Mary and Joseph, kneeling on the scattered straw. In the background, a single, clear voice began to sing "Silent Night, Holy Night."

Suddenly the room stilled. It was as if the holiness of that first Christmas had somehow transcended two millennia and now filled the little church in California. Audrey Mieir writes: "The atmosphere was charged. I so often have thought that I could hear the rustling of angels' wings. It seemed that the whole room was filled with the presence of the angels of God." As she looked around the room she realized she was not alone in this perception. Tears shone in the eyes of many of the older church members, and little children sat transfixed, watching the tranquil scene while the soloist's pure voice carried them back to that first Christmas night.

When the echo of the last line, "sleep in heavenly peace," faded, the pastor stood. Without a word, he slowly raised his arms toward heaven and then stood for just a moment before proclaiming in a loud voice, "His name is Wonderful!" It was as if the words electrified Audrey. Quickly she grabbed her Bible and turned to the concordance, searching for the various names given to Jesus by the writers of Scripture. Hastily, she jotted the words and phrases she discovered: Wonderful Counselor, Lord, King, Mighty God, Shepherd, Rock, Prince of Peace. Before long she had a list written in the back of her Bible. She read and reread the names for Jesus, thinking that there must be a reason for her urgency. God must have a message for her to share. A woman of prayer, Audrey quietly asked the Lord to reveal His will.

Later that evening, she composed a simple chorus and included many of the titles from her hastily-written list. She sat down at the piano and began to play and sing the verses God had given in answer to her prayer. Immediately, the young people gathered around the piano, picked up the melody, and began to sing along. Within a short time, the simple praise chorus, composed during the Christmas program at the Bethel Union Church, was being sung in churches and in neighboring communities. Later that year it was published. Since that time, "His Name Is Wonderful" has been translated into many different languages and included in songbooks and hymnals in several countries. What began as a Christmas gift to one woman in a small church in California has become a blessing to millions of Christians throughout the world.

His Name Is Wonderful

Audrey Mieir   Audrey Mieir

His name is Won-der-ful, His name is Won-der-ful, His name is Won-der-ful,

Je-sus, my Lord; He is the might-y King, Mas-ter of ev-'ry-thing,

His name is Won-der-ful, Je-sus, my Lord. He's the great Shep-herd, the Rock of all

a-ges, Al-might-y God is He; Bow down be-fore Him,

Love and a-dore Him, His name is Won-der-ful, Je-sus, my Lord. Lord.

The God of Abraham Praise

Thomas Olivers, 1725—1799

A SONG FROM A SHOEMAKER

When he was only four years old, Thomas Olivers was orphaned. His relatives saw the little boy as an unwanted burden and looked for a way to be rid of him. Passed from family to family, Thomas never knew the love and security of a real home. Before he was ten years old, his relatives bound him out as an apprentice to a shoemaker in his hometown of Tregonan, England. But Thomas's unhappy childhood had toughened him. He had learned to survive by taking care of himself in any way he could. Before long he had distinguished himself as one of the "worst characters" in town. He hung around the pubs, got into fights, stole as often as he could get away with it, and cheated the customers in the cobbler's shop. By the time he was in his mid-twenties, he was run out of town as a "ne'er do well."

In the summer of 1752, Thomas Olivers was living and working in Bristol when he heard that the famous evangelist George Whitefield was in town. The young shoemaker decided to go hear Whitefield preach. Determined to get a good view of the celebrity, Olivers arrived for the meeting early and stood waiting in the August sun for three hours. Years later, in a letter to a friend, Olivers recounted the event as follows: "When the sermon began, I was certainly a dreadful enemy of God and to all that is good;

and one of the most profligate and abandoned young men living." But then the preacher spoke of God's desire to rescue those who are in danger of being consumed by sin. He used as his text Zechariah 3:2, where the Lord refers to such a one as a "brand plucked out of the fire." When the young shoe-maker heard these words, it was as if they gripped him by the heart. He left the meeting deeply convicted of his own sinfulness. After several days in anguished soul-searching and prayer, Thomas Olivers surrendered his life to God and found the peace and acceptance for which he had longed.

Determined to make a complete break with his former lifestyle, Olivers sold what little he had, bought a horse, and traveled around the countryside. Everywhere he went, he fearlessly preached about the power of God and his own amazing conversion. Before long, he joined the Methodist Society and met the well-known Methodist revivalist John Wesley. Wesley recognized the fervor and courage of the preaching shoemaker, and he challenged Olivers to serve with him as a traveling evangelist. It was a call Olivers joyfully answered, and before long he was crisscrossing England and Ireland on horseback, preaching and teaching to all who would listen. It has been recorded that Olivers traveled over 100,000 miles bringing the gospel of Christ to thousands.

On one of his trips to London in 1770, Olivers stayed with a friend, John Bakewell, who resided in Westminster. It was here that Olivers wrote his famous hymn "The God of Abraham Praise." One day he decided to visit the Great Synagogue at Duke's Place in London. He arrived in time to hear the cantor sing the *Yigdal*—a paraphrase of the thirteen articles of the Jewish faith. The *Yigdal* had been composed three hundred years earlier, but the words and haunting melody so impacted Olivers that he determined to make a translation suitable for use by a Christian congregation. Despite his lack of formal training in either poetry or music, Olivers wrote twelve verses to his adaptation of the ancient Jewish melody. He entitled his poem, "A Hymn to the God of Abraham." His work was not immediately recognized by many of his contemporaries, who suggested that he should stick to his trade of cobbling and leave the writing of hymns to those with better training. Since that time, however, this majestic hymn has been praised by great poets, including Ralph Waldo Emerson, who described it as "the greatest hymn in the English language."

Although his humble and notorious beginnings were seen by some as a stain upon his character and work, many others found in Thomas Olivers a shining example of the redemptive work of Christ. For more than fifty years, the shoemaker-turned-preacher faithfully delivered his message; and when he died in London in 1799, he was buried in John Wesley's tomb in City Road Chapel burying ground. The once unwanted orphan had found his final resting place among those belonging to the family of God.

The God of Abraham Praise

Thomas Olivers   Meyer Lyon

1. The God of A - br'ham praise, Who reigns en-throned a - bove,
2. He by Him - self hath sworn, We on His oath de - pend;
3. The God who reigns on high The great arch - an - gels sing,
4. The whole tri - um - phant host Give thanks to God on high;

The An - cient of e - ter - nal days, And God of love.
We shall, on ea - gles' wings up - borne, To heav'n as - cend;
And "Ho - ly, ho - ly, ho - ly" cry, "Al - might - y King!"
"Hail, Fa - ther, Son and Ho - ly Ghost!" They ev - er cry.

Je - ho - vah, great I AM, By earth and heav'n con - fessed:
We shall be - hold His face, We shall His pow'r a - dore,
Who was and is the same, And ev - er - more shall be:
Hail, A - br'ham's God and mine! With heav'n our songs we raise;

We bow and bless the sa - cred name For - ev - er blest.
And sing the won - ders of His grace For - ev - er - more.
E - ter - nal Fa - ther, great I AM, We wor - ship Thee.
All might and maj - es - ty are Thine, And end - less praise.

The Church's One Foundation
Samuel J. Stone, 1839–1900

A HYMN TO BATTLE HERESY

Although the Bible states that the "meek shall inherit the earth," the church has seen its share of courageous fighters. At different times, whether threatened from without or within, men and women have gone to battle for their faith. Spears, arrows, swords, and guns are the more customary weapons, but in the mid-nineteenth century a hymn was used very effectively to defeat an enemy of the church.

In 1863, the Anglican church was rocked to its foundations by books written by one of its influential bishops, John William Colenso of Natal. In his commentaries on both the Old and New Testaments, the liberal Anglican distanced himself from the orthodox views of Christ and the Scriptures. When his volume questioning the historical accuracy of the first five books of the Bible was published, Colenso was labeled an enemy of the Church. Forty other bishops signed a letter requesting his resignation; and when he traveled to England from his post in Africa, he was refused access to Anglican pulpits and threatened with excommunication.

During the time of this great controversy, a London pastor, Samuel J. Stone, ministered to the city's East End. Known as the poor man's pastor, Stone was primarily concerned with the spiritual condition of the weak and destitute among his parishioners. Although he was known for his tender heart and compassionate nature, Stone also had a tenacious spirit and never shrank from defending his faith. When he read the words of Colenso and a rebutting article by Bishop Gray of Capetown, Samuel Stone determined to compose a work that would affirm the basic doctrines of the Bible and the undeniable lordship of Jesus Christ. Instead of devoting himself to a scholarly treatise or a theological debate, the "poor man's pastor" turned to poetry. For his subject matter he chose the Apostles' Creed and specifically directed his attention to the ninth article, which addresses the universality of the church, the communion of saints, and the assertion that Christ is the Head of the body (or church).

The result of his defense of the faith was written and published in 1866 as the hymn, "The Church's One Foundation." In it Stone intertwines the biblical imagery of the church as the bride of Christ with the doctrines of salvation, baptism, communion, and redemption. Originally containing seven stanzas, the hymn effectively denied every heresy put forth by Bishop Colenso.

Samuel Stone's hymn was set to a melody composed by Samuel S. Wesley, the grandson of Charles Wesley, and was immediately embraced as the theme of those holding to the traditional view of Scripture at that time. When the conservative Anglican bishops assembled in London for a conference in 1868, they chose "The Church's One Foundation" as their processional as well as their theme hymn.

Stone went on to author more than a half-dozen books of verse and numerous hymns in the years following, but none ever reached the popularity of his first hymn. In it, he blended faith and passion in a way that touched both the hearts and minds of the faithful. When the courageous pastor died in 1900, at the age of sixty-one, it could accurately be said that he had "fought the good fight"—not with swords or guns, but with a hymn.

In thee, O Lord, do I put my trust;
let me never be ashamed: deliver me in thy righteousness.
Bow down thine ear to me; deliver me speedily:
be thou my strong rock, for an house of defense to save me.
For thou art my rock and my fortress; therefore
for thy name's sake lead me, and guide me. *Psalm 31:1–3*

The Church's One Foundation

Samuel J. Stone   Samuel S. Wesley

1. The Church-'s one foun-da-tion Is Je-sus Christ, her Lord;
2. E-lect from ev-'ry na-tion, Yet one o'er all the earth;
3. 'Mid toil and trib-u-la-tion And tu-mult of her war,
4. Yet she on earth hath un-ion With God, the Three in One,

She is His new cre-a-tion By wa-ter and the Word;
Her char-ter of sal-va-tion, One Lord, one faith, one birth;
She waits the con-sum-ma-tion Of peace for-ev-er-more;
And mys-tic sweet com-mu-nion With those whose rest is won;

From heav'n He came and sought her To be His ho-ly bride;
One ho-ly name she bless-es, Par-takes one ho-ly food,
Till, with the vi-sion glo-rious, Her long-ing eyes are blest,
O hap-py ones and ho-ly! Lord, give us grace that we

With His own blood He bought her, And for her life He died.
And to one hope she press-es, With ev-'ry grace en-dued.
And the great church vic-to-rious Shall be the church at rest.
Like them, the meek and low-ly, On high may dwell with Thee.

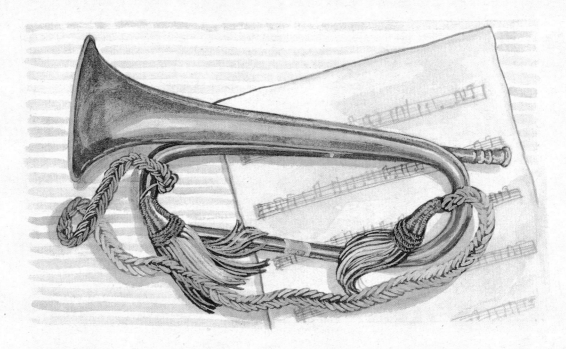

Taps
Daniel Adams Butterfield, 1831–1901

TWENTY-FOUR NOTES ON A BUGLE

Although not strictly a hymn, the strains of "Taps" are probably the most recognizable twenty-four notes in our country's musical history. The eloquent and haunting melody has drifted over the graves of soldiers since it was first played by a lone bugler on a Civil War battlefield in 1862.

It was mid-summer and the Union and Confederate armies had been fighting for seven long days at Harrison's Landing in Virginia. Brigadier General Daniel A. Butterfield was serving as commander of a brigade of the Fifth Corps of the Army of the Potomac. The fighting had been brutal and the troops on each side had suffered considerable loss. At that time, the only efficient way for leaders to communicate with their troops was with the use of bugle calls designated for specific purposes. There were calls for charge, retreat, lights out, and other orders. On this particular evening, Butterfield contemplated the traditional tattoo, or taps, used to signal lights out. He felt it was too rigid and not melodic enough to signal the end of the day. Unable to write music, he composed a variation of the tattoo in his head, called in someone who could write down the notes as he whistled them, and had him jot down the melody on the back of an envelope. Then Butterfield sent for his brigade bugler, Oliver W. Norton. Together they tinkered with the melodic line until the general was satisfied. At the end of their meeting, Butterfield directed Norton to substitute the new call for taps from that evening on. Norton wrote in a letter to a reporter several years later:

> The music was beautiful on that still summer night and was heard far beyond the limits of our Brigade. The next day I was visited by several buglers from neighboring brigades, asking for copies of the music which I gladly furnished. I think no general order was issued from army headquarters authorizing the substitution of this for the regulation call, but as each brigade commander exercised his own discretion in such minor matters, the call was gradually taken up through the Army of the Potomac.

The bugle call was initially intended to signal the setting of the sun, but the tradition of playing "Taps" at military funerals began very shortly after its composition. Captain John C. Tidball of the Union army was charged with supervising the burial of his cannoneer killed in action during the Peninsular Campaign at Harrison's Landing. At that time, the custom was to fire three rifle shots over the grave at the close of the funeral service. But Tidball's troops were concealed in the woods in an advanced position. He feared that the firing of three volleys so near enemy forces might renew fighting and so decided to substitute the sounding of "Taps" as a tribute to the fallen comrade. Before long, the custom was carried throughout the Army of the Potomac until it was eventually confirmed by orders as the official tribute at the grave of any fallen serviceman.

It seems fitting that a melody played most often at times of great human drama be sung both to mark the close of a day and to reflect on the close of a life. At the end of the day, as well as at the end of a life, there is the longing for assurance that "all is well for God is nigh."

For he hath said, I will never leave thee, nor forsake thee. So that we may boldly say, The Lord is my helper, and I will not fear what man shall do unto me. Hebrews 13:5-6

Taps

Daniel Adams Butterfield   Oliver W. Norton

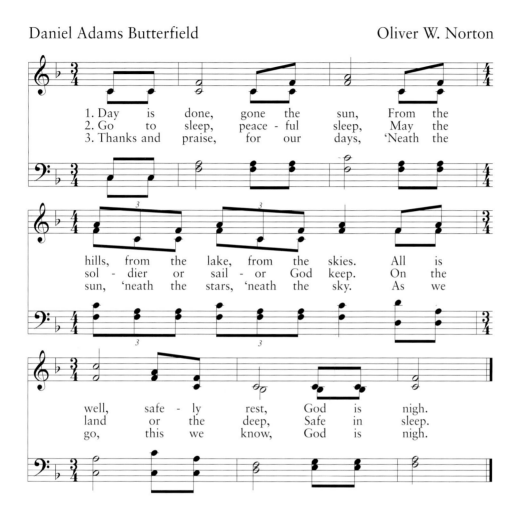

1. Day is done, gone the sun, From the
2. Go to sleep, peace - ful sleep, May the
3. Thanks and praise, for our days, 'Neath the

hills, from the lake, from the skies. All is
sol - dier or sail - or God keep. On the
sun, 'neath the stars, 'neath the sky. As we

well, safe - ly rest, God is nigh.
land or the deep, Safe in sleep.
go, this we know, God is nigh.

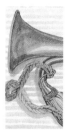

157

Taps

*Whither shall I go from thy spirit? or whither shall
I flee from thy presence? If I take the wings of
the morning, and dwell in the uttermost parts
of the sea; Even there shall thy hand lead me,
and thy right hand shall hold me. If I say,
Surely the darkness shall cover me; even the night
shall be light about me. Yea, the darkness hideth not
from thee; but the night shineth as the day: the darkness
and the light are both alike to thee.   Psalm 139:7, 9-12*

But be filled with the Spirit; Speaking to
yourselves in psalms and hymns and spiritual songs,
singing and making melody in your heart
to the Lord; Giving thanks always
for all things unto God and the Father
in the name of our Lord Jesus Christ. *Ephesians 5:18-20*

HYMN TITLE INDEX

Author and Composer Index

First Line Index

Photography Locations

Pages 2-3: Snowmass Wilderness, Colorado. 5: Snowmass Wilderness, Colorado. 8: Seashore State Park, Virginia. 12: Wrangell-Saint Elias National Park & Preserve, Alaska. 16: Porcupine Mountains Wilderness State Park, Michigan. 20: Hanging Lake, Colorado. 24: Klamath Range, California. 28: Jasper National Park, Alberta, Canada. 32: Catskill Mountains, New York. 34-35: Denali National Park, Alaska. 38: Fremont Peak State Park, California. 42: Monterey Peninsula, California. 47: Independence Pass, Colorado. 51: Temblor Range, California. 54: Sierra Nevada, California. 58: Northern Sierra Nevada, California. 62: Grand Canyon National Park, Arizona. 64: Big Sur Coast, California. 69: Zion National Park, Utah. 72: Antelope Valley, California. 76: Glacier National Park, Montana. 80: Northern Sierra Nevada, California. 84: Monterey Peninsula, California. 89: Guadalupe Mountains National Park, Texas. 92: Eastern Sierra Nevada, California. 96: Carmel Valley, California. 98-99: Antelope Valley, California. 102: Organ Pipe Cactus National Monument, Arizona. 107: Northern Sierra Nevada, California. 110: Prince William Sound, Alaska. 114: San Rafael Desert, Utah. 118: Yosemite National Park, California. 122: Organ Pipe Cactus National Monument, Arizona. 126: Adirondack Park & Preserve, New York. 128-29: McArthur-Burney Falls Memorial State Park, California. 132: Trinidad State Beach, California. 136: Sequoia National Park, California. 140: Adirondack Park & Preserve, New York. 144: Yosemite National Park, California. 148: Grafton Notch State Park, Maine. 152: Northern Monongahela National Forest, West Virginia. 156: Lake Superior, Michigan.